DIRTY KOREAN

SECOND EDITION

DIRTY KOREAN

Spice Up Your Conversation *with* Casual Slang to Use with Friends, Enemies, Lovers, *and More*

SECOND EDITION

HAEWON BAEK
& JINNY BAEK

Published by
ULYSSES PRESS
an imprint of The Stable Book Group
32 Court Street, Suite 2109
Brooklyn, NY 11201
www.ulyssespress.com

Library of Congress Control Number: 2025933928
ISBN: 978-1-64604-771-0
eISBN: 978-1-64604-772-7

Project editor: Kierra Sondereker
Managing editor: Claire Chun
Editor: Phyllis Elving
English proofreader: Renee Rutledge
Korean proofreader: Corey Colling
Production: Abbey Gregory
Front cover design: Akangksha Sarmah
Cover artwork: Freepik except mochi © Mariia Petrova/shutterstock.com, shot glasses © Kirill.Veretennikov/shutterstock.com, lips © mentalmind/shutterstock.com, back cover squiggles © redgreystock/shutterstock.com

Printed in the United States
10 9 8 7 6 5 4 3 2 1

For my husband, who adores my silliness, and my children, 백산 백솔 백샘, who make me insane from time to time to help me appreciate life. I love you guys.

—Haewon Baek

This book is dedicated to my sister for giving me the chance to cowrite this book, as well as my family for the support ♥. I love all of you.

—Jinny Baek

CONTENTS

USING THIS BOOK

Whether you're an exchange student headed to Korea to study and broaden your worldview or a frat bro looking to drink your ass off and meet the fine ladies of Korea, you're gonna need to know more than just how to say "hi" and "thank you." You'll need to be able to order a drink, pick up a date, and tell a douchebag to "go the fuck away"—which would be a simple *gguh juh* (꺼져).

This book is designed to teach you those sorts of words, the ones your professors were too scared to teach you, those phrases too raunchy to appear in any textbook, and all those expressions you would never, ever say in front of your mother—in short, all the sayings that you actually give a shit about. Because let's be honest, when was the last time you were hanging out with friends and felt the need to say "I live in the red house. I enjoy tennis. Where is the library?" Nobody talks this way, least of all Koreans, who—once they warm up to you—can be some of the most foulmouthed motherfuckers you'll ever meet. So let's get real for a change.

Dirty Korean is the product of a lifetime of vulgar language picked up from lots of bad company and many a poor life choice—none of which is regretted today, however, because it all led to this little gem of a book that is now passed on to you, dear reader. Use it wisely and at your own peril.

The content has been arranged thematically, and each English phrase is followed by the Korean pronunciation and written characters. Important and interesting tidbits on Korean culture have been included to give you a better understanding of the phrases, places, and social customs you'll encounter during your travels. That's because we'd hate to have you mistake a sarcastic pickup line for a verbal slap-in-the-face and lose your chance at baggin' some hottie. So go forth—take your *Dirty Korean* and get dirty with it!

•••••Quick-and-Dirty Korean Pronunciation

Korean is super easy to read and write once you master the 24 characters that, when put together, make up the sounds of the Korean language. If you're a quick learner, you'll probably master them in about an hour. The letters consist of geometric shapes that were created by King Sejong in the 1400s.

TONES

To most foreigners, Korean just sounds angry or whiny. Koreans tend to speak with a stiff intonation, as opposed to using the more fluid sounds of English speakers. One way to practice your Korean accent is to drag your tongue at the end of your syllables to make the sounds a little whinier (the tilde after the hangeul means you should drag out the syllable).

> **Hello~**
> *Annyeong~*
> 안녕~

CONSONANTS

The Korean alphabet has 14 consonants that are similar to those in English. However, double consonants are pronounced differently. They should be spoken with a strong emphasis that almost makes you sound angry.

ㄱ = **g**, **k**, as in "gorgeous" / ㄲ = gg

ㄴ = **n**, as in "norm"

ㄷ = **d**, **t**, as in "drum" / ㄸ = dd, tt

ㄹ = **r**, **l**, as in "rude"

ㅁ = **m**, as in "morning"

ㅂ = **b**, **p**, as in "breasts" / ㅃ = pp like in "pepper"

ㅅ = **s**, as in "sex"/ㅆ = ss

ㅇ = **ng**, as in "meeting" (but silent if at the beginning of the word)

ㅈ = **j**, as in "joy"/ㅉ = jj

ㅊ = **ch**, as in "chihuahua"

ㅋ = **k**, as in "key"

ㅌ = **t**, as in "toy"

ㅍ = **p**, as in "punch"

ㅎ = **h**, as in "horny"

VOWELS

The Korean dialect has 10 vowels. It can be difficult to pronounce them at first because of how similar they sound. But once you get the hang of it, it's pretty easy.

ㅏ = **a**, as in "father"

ㅑ = **ya**, as in "yahoo"

ㅓ = **eo**, as in "fuck"

ㅕ = **yeo**, as in "y'all"

ㅗ = **oh**, as in "old"

ㅛ = **yo**, as in "yo mama"

ㅜ = **u**, as in "moon"

ㅠ = **yu**, as in "you"

ㅡ = **eu**; there is no sound like this in English. Just put your teeth together and pull your lips while you try to make this vowel sound.

ㅣ = **i**, as in "lily" or "silly"

Also, Korean vowels combine to make different sounds, such as,

ㅐ (ㅏ + ㅣ) = **ae**, as in "bayer"

ㅒ (ㅑ + ㅣ) = **yae**, as in "yeah"

ㅔ (ㅓ + ㅣ) = **e**, as in "never"

ㅖ (ㅕ + ㅣ) = **ye**, as in "Yale"

ㅘ (ㅗ + ㅏ) = **wa**, as in "wash"

ㅙ (ㅗ + ㅐ) = **wae**, as in "whey"

ㅚ (ㅗ + ㅣ) = **oe**, also as in "whey"

ㅝ (ㅜ + ㅓ) = **wo**, as in "woman"

ㅞ (ㅜ + ㅔ) = **we**, as in "wedding"

ㅟ (ㅜ + ㅣ) = **wi**, as in "wing"

ㅢ (ㅡ + ㅣ) = **ui**, as in "ooh-ee"

Just know that even if you know how to read each character correctly, what people actually say won't sound the way you'd imagine it. Just as in English, Korean words have a liaison, making sentences easier to read—but unfortunately for you, more difficult to say. Well, you can thank us for putting the pronunciation right there for you to see, so you can sound it out just the way the phrases are used in real life!

HOW TO READ KOREAN

Korean can be written in either the standard Western style (left to right in horizontal rows) or in vertical columns reading from top to bottom and right to left, though the latter is rarely used nowadays.

When reading the characters, remember that letters (consonants and vowels) never stand alone—consonants are always combined with a vowel (or a vowel and another consonant) to form syllable blocks. These blocks always start with a consonant, followed by a vowel to the right or below it. Note: When the consonant "ㅇ" is placed at the beginning of a block, it's silent.

You pronounce the sound of the letters in a syllable block from left to right first, then read any letters that are at the bottom half of the block. The bottom letters are called *batchim* (받침), supporting consonants used at the end of the syllable block to form the sound. For example, 한글 (hangeul) reads as follows:

ㅎ (h)

ㅏ (a)

ㄴ (n)

ㄱ (g)

ㅡ (eu)

ㄹ (l)

Then try to pronounce 쉽다 (*swipda*) = ㅅ (s), ㅟ (wi), ㅂ (p), ㄷ (d), ㅏ (a). You just said 한글쉽다—which means "Korean is easy!" The learning's gonna be so fast that you'll be drinking a bottle of soju and haggling with a prostitute in no time!

CHAPTER 1

HOWDY KOREAN

HANGUK INSAMAL

한국 인사말

••••• Hello

Annyeonghaseyo

안녕하세요

Unlike the case with some languages, it's cool to use Korean slang with complete strangers—but only if you're older than they are. If you're not, or if it's questionable, you'd best stick to formalities and old-fashioned "hellos." Korea is age-deferential like that. If you're with friends, though, all bets are off—feel free to get as slangy as you wanna be.

Hi (to someone your age or younger)
Annyeong
안녕

Yo!
Ya!
야!

Hey!
Imma!
임마!

•••••On the phone

Hello?
Yeoboseyo?
여보세요?

Who dis?
Nuguseyo?
누구세요?

•••••What's up?
Wannya? / Wasseo?
왔냐? / 왔어?

Just know that whenever they see you, Koreans—especially older people—will ask you if you've eaten. That's their way of asking "How are you?" So just answer "yes" and ask them if they've eaten as well.

Have you eaten?
Bap mugun-ni?
밥 먹었니?

I've already eaten.
Muguh-ssuyo.
먹었어요.

Not yet.
Ahjik-ee-yo.
아직이요.

Do you want something to eat?
Muh jom mugl-le?
뭐 좀 먹을래?

That's okay.
Gwenchanayo.
괜찮아요.

Have you eaten? (to older people)
Siksa hashussuyo?
식사 하셨어요?

As in any language, you always gotta find out how your peeps been doin' when you haven't seen 'em in a while. Don't be too surprised, though, when Koreans talk bluntly about how fat your ass has gotten since they last saw you. Changes to your physical appearance are considered fair game for discussion. Don't be offended. It is what it is, fatty.

How ya been?
Jal jinaeni?
잘 지내니?

Yeah, I'm good!
Eung, jal jinae!
응, 잘 지내!

Good!
Joa!
좋아!

So-so.
Geunyang geurae.
그냥 그래.

Whatcha been up to?
Mohago sarannya?
뭐하고 살았냐?

Long time no see!
Orenmaniya!
오랜만이야

Let's grab something to eat.
Bob hanbun mukjja.
밥 한번 먹자.

This is for when you can't stay and talk for a long time. It doesn't mean you have to grab something to eat in real life—it's just a way of saying hi.

You're still alive?
Saraisseonnya?
살아있었냐?

You need to lose some weight!
Sal jom bbaeyagetda!
살 좀 빼야겠다!

Your face has gotten chubbier!
Eolguri tongtonghae!
얼굴이 통통해!

•••••Goodbye

Jal jinae~
잘 지내~

You know how in Hawaii "aloha" means both "hi" and "bye"? Well, Korean is the same way. You just have to drag out the end of the Korean word for "hello" to say "bye."

Goodbye (general use)
Annyeong~
안녕~

Goodbye (to a person staying)
Jal isseo~
잘 있어~

Goodbye (to a person leaving)
Jal ga~
잘 가~

Goodbye (when both parties are parting)
Jal jinae~
잘 지내~
Literally, "be well."

Bye-bye
Bai bai
바이 바이

See ya!
Tho boja!
또 보자!

Later!
Najungebwa!
나중에봐!

I'm out.
Na ganda.
나 간다.

Be careful!
Josimhae!
조심해!

•••••G'morning!
Joeun achim!
좋은 아침!

The formal ways of saying "good morning" and "good evening" are so long-winded that you might pass out trying to say them in one breath. Better not to risk it. Stick with the more casual ways of greeting friends and family.

Good morning (formal)
Annyeonghi jumusyeoseoyo
안녕히 주무셨어요?

G'morning!
Joeun achim!
좋은 아침!

Did you sleep well?
Jal jasseo?
잘잤어?

Good evening (formal)
Annyeonghi jumuseyo
안녕히 주무세요

Evenin'
Jaja~
잘자~

G'night
goodbam
굿밤

Sweet dreams!
Joeun kkumkkwo!
좋은 꿈꿔!

Dream about me!
Nae kkumkkwo!
내 꿈꿔!

•••••I am sorry
Mianhapnida
미안합니다

Let's be honest. Apologizing blows—and you usually don't even mean it. But it's one of those things that you need to know how to do, even if it's bullshit. And if you have to do it, you might as well have some fun with it.

I apologize. (formal)
Jwesonghapnida.
죄송합니다.

Sorry! (informal)
Mian!
미안!

Forgive me!
Yongseohaejwo!
용서해줘!

Oops!
At!
앗!

EXCUSE ME

SILLYEHAMNIDA / JAMSIMANYO

실례합니다 / 잠시만요

"Excuse me" can be used as an apology or to request a favor. But don't worry about saying "excuse me" every time you bump into someone in Korea. It's a small country packed with people. Shit happens. Just keep walking and pretend it never happened. Also, don't get offended if some ol' ladies (*ajummas*) bump into you or cut you off when you're in line for the subway. They've been trained to be like that through their entire existence. Be the better person and smile! Or you can cuss them out and give them the finger. Your choice.

Excuse me
Sillyehamnida / Jamsimanyo
실례합니다 / 잠시만요
Literally, "one minute," but you can use this one to get through the crazy crowds in Korea.

Move out of my way!
Bikyeo!
비켜!

Be careful!
Josimhe!
조심해!

No worries.
Geokjeonghajima~.
걱정하지마~.

It's all good.
Gwaenchana.
괜찮아.

No problem.
Munjae eopsseo.
문제없어.

Forget about it.
Ijeobeoryeo.
잊어버려.

Well, excuuuuse me for living!
Jugeuljoereuljyeotda!
죽을 죄를 졌다!
Literally, "I have committed a killing sin!" said sarcastically—as in "I'm soooo sorry for what I've done to deserve to DIE!"

••••• Please

Budi / Jebal
부디 / 제발

Koreans don't really use the word "please" except in an extremely formal setting or out of sheer desperation ("Please don't sodomize me with that rusty ice pick, sir"). Because "please" isn't used much in their language, Koreans are often thought to be rude or demanding when they're in the States. But they're not—it's just their language.

Can you please scratch my back?
Nae deung ***jom*** *geulgeojullae?*
내 등 **좀** 긁어줄래?
When Koreans ask for something politely, they say the word "little" (*jom*; 좀) instead of please.

Can you please do me a favor?
*Budi butak **jom** deureojullae?*
부디 부탁 **좀** 들어줄래?

INTRODUCING YOURSELF

JAGI SOGAE

자기 소개

My name is James.
Nae ireumeun James ipnida.
내 이름은 제임스 입니다.

I am from America.
Jeoneun migook eseo wasseupnida.
저는 미국에서 왔습니다.

I have yellow fever.
Jeoneun donyanginman joahapnida.
저는 동양인만 좋아합니다.

I am 18 years old and full of testosterone.
Jeoneun yeollyeodeolssaligo himi neomchipnida.
저는 열여덟살이고 힘이 넘칩니다.

I like hairy girls.
Jeoneun teol maneun yeojaga josseupnida.
저는 털 많은 여자가 좋습니다.

••••••Making friends

Chingu mandeulgi

친구 만들기

If you want to make friends in Korea, don't go up to strangers and just start talking to them. That's creepy. Instead, you can meet people through internet clubs (such as meetup.com) or Facebook events. Also, you can make friends at different clubs in the Hongdae or Itaewon areas of Seoul while you get drunk and dance with strangers. If you're a guy looking to hook up, clubs are definitely the way to go. Korean girls will throw themselves at you if you're a foreigner. They want to learn English and consider the big sausages a bonus. Show them what you've got! It's easier to get laid if you have friends to back you up. So take your fugly wingmen out with you to take the fugly girls out of the equation.

Group Date
Miting
미팅
These are occasions when a bunch of girls and boys—usually high schoolers or college students—meet for a date.

Hey, is there a group date you can set up?
*Ya, **miting**jari eopsseo?*
야, **미팅**자리 없어?

Do you have someone you picked?
Jjigeun ae isseo?
찍은 애 있어?

Blind date
Sogaeting
소개팅

Can you set me up on a blind date with one of your hottie friends?
*Jal saeng-gin chingurang na **sogaeting** sikyeojo?*
잘 생긴 친구랑 나 **소개팅** 시켜줘.

She/he is my type.
Wahn nae seu
완내스

She/he is not my type.
Ccalmi
깔미

Arranged blind date for marriage
Seon
선
A long time ago, all Koreans had arranged marriages. Although most people marry out of love nowadays, a few Koreans are

still forced by their parents to go through arranged blind dates to meet the "right partner."

Nice to meet you.
Mannaseo ban-gapseupnida.
만나서 반갑습니다.

What's your name?
Ireumi mwoyeyo?
이름이 뭐예요?

Have we met before?
Uri mannanjeok itnayo?
우리 만난적 있나요?

Do you have the time?
Jigeum myeossiyeyo?
지금 몇시예요?

How old are you?
Naiga eotteoke dwae?
나이가 어떻게 돼?

In Korea, you are considered to be one year old as soon as you pop out of your mom's vajay. If you are born on the last day of the year, December 31, then the very next day you will turn two years old. So don't forget to add one year when you are sharing your age in Korea.

Really? You don't look that old!
Jeongmal? Geureoke an boyeo~!
정말? 그렇게 안 보여~!

Me, too! I'm the same age!
Nado! dong-gap!
나도 동갑!

Let's not talk so formally.
Uri mal noeulkkayo? / Mal pyunagyehae.
우리 말 놓을까요? / 말 편하게 해.

Do you come here often?
Yeogi jajuwa?
여기 자주와?

Do you want to get a drink?
Uri sul hanjan halkka?
우리 술 한잔 할까?

Where are you from?
Eodiseo wasseo?
어디서 왔어?

Where do you live?
Eodi sara?
어디 살아?

Let's be friends.
Uri chingu halkka?
우리 친구 할까?

What's your cell phone number?
Haenponbeonhoga mwoya?
핸폰번호가 뭐야?

Do you have Instagram?
Insta issuh?
인스타 있어?

Can I text you on KakaoTalk?
Ka-tok haedo dae?
카톡해도 돼?
All Korean people have an app called KakaoTalk. If you plan on visiting South Korea, you might want to download the app and register so you can use Kakao Taxi. South Koreans don't use Uber or Lyft. Kakao Taxi works the best, and you can prepay by credit card or in person.

Wanna go have sex?
Uri enjoy halkka?
우리 인조이 할까?
Literally, "let's enjoy tonight."

•••••Pictures

Sajin

사진

Ever since the digital camera revolution, Koreans have become obsessed with taking pictures. You'll have to be patient when they take pics of their meals before eating at restaurants, which has become something of a tradition. You can't touch the food before the girls take pictures of it— they'll chop your hands off, so be careful! And if you want to take a photo of some of your Korean friends, know that Koreans have a huge complex about their head or face size. It's common to see people fight over who gets to stand in the background to make their head look smaller than everybody else's. That's also why you might see people covering their cheeks with their hand or bangs. And when you strike a pose, don't forget to make the V-for-victory sign with your hand before the shutter snaps!

Self-taking picture skill
Selka
셀카
Yes, Koreans have a word for this. Even with their short arms they can get about four to five people in a selfie, including themselves. They say the best angle for taking selfies is 45 degrees above your face.

Cell phone camera
Ponka
폰카

Let's take a picture!
Sajin jjikja!
사진 찍자!

Can you take a picture of me?
Sajin jjigeo juseyo.
사진 찍어 주세요.

Can you get everything in the background?
Dwi-eh da na-o-gye jjiguhjooseyo.
뒤에 다 나오게 찍어주세요.

Make me look tall.
Giruh bo-i-gye jjiguhjo.
길어 보이게 찍어줘.

One, two, three
Hana, dul, set
하나 둘 셋

Cheese
Kimchi~
김치~
Saying "kimchi" is like saying "cheese" when taking a picture in Korea. You can say it to make the perfect smiling face in a picture. This is a must-do—along with the V-for-victory (or peace sign)—when you take pictures.

CHAPTER 2

FRIENDLY KOREAN

HANGUK CHINGUKKIRI HANEUNMAL

한국 친구끼리 하는말

If your only impression of Koreans is the Hollywood portrayal of a pissed-off liquor store owner with a gun, you may think all Koreans have a bug up their ass. You'd be wrong—Koreans are warm and affectionate people...once you get to know them. But first you'll have to break through the sometimes forceful and angry sounds of the language. If you can do that, you'll find yourself well on your way to forming some lasting friendships.

•••••Friends

Chingudeul

친구들

Most Koreans have a ton of friends and acquaintances, and they have a pupu platter of words used to describe those different relationships. It's no different in the States, really. After all, here you've got your BF or GF, your BFF, your booty call, your homies, your Facebook friends, and, of course, your *World of Warcraft* avatar friends—who aren't actually real people, let alone real friends.

Friend
Chingu
친구

Are you my real friend?
*Neo jinjja nae **chingu** maja?*
너 진짜 내 **친구** 맞아?

Total stranger
Moreuneun saram / Cheoeum bon saram
모르는 사람 / 처음 본 사람

That total stranger smiled all creepy at me!
***Cheom bo neun sarami** nabogo jingeurupge useosseo!*
첨 보는 사람이 나보고 징그럽게 웃었어!

Acquaintance
Aneun saram
아는 사람

She's just an acquaintance from school.
*Hakgyoeseo geunyang **aneun saramiya.***
학교에서 그냥 **아는 사람**이야.

Classmate
Ban chingu
반 친구

Coworker
Hoesa dongryo
회사동료

My coworker is slacking off and giving me all his work.
*Nae **hoesa dong**iga jakku ireul nahante tteo neomgyeo.*
내 **회사 동기**가 자꾸 일을 나한테 떠 넘겨.

Homie
Bural chingu
불알 친구
Literally, "testicle friends"—i.e., you've been friends since you were babies, when it was all good to see each other's nutsacks. (To be used among men only.)

> **He's my homie.**
> *Nae **bural chingu**ya.*
> 내 **불알친구**야.

Next-door neighbor
Yeopjip chingu / iut
옆집 친구 / 이웃

> **My next-door neighbor is like family.**
> *Nae yupjip sarameun nae **iut sachon**iji.*
> 내 옆집사람은 내 **이웃사촌**이지.
> Literally, "neighbor cousin."

Friends from the same neighborhood
Dongne chingu
동네 친구

Study buddy
Gateun gwa chingu
같은 과 친구
This is used for university students, referring to friends with the same major.

School friend
Hakgyo chingu
학교 친구

Housemate
Dongeoin
동거인

My housemate farts all day long.
*Nae **dongeoin** bangu mennal kkyeo.*
내 **동거인** 방구 맨날껴.

BFF (mainly used by girls in grade school)
Danjjak
단짝

Best friend
Jeil chinhan chingu
제일 친한 친구

Partner (someone who sits next to you in grade school)
Jjakgung
짝궁
In Korean elementary schools, students sit two abreast in assigned seats. You're stuck with your partner for a whole semester unless the teacher decides to make a seating change. This leads to territorial behavior for your rightful half of the desk, usually demarcated by an invisible line you draw smack dab in the middle. So if your eraser crosses into your partner's domain, the eraser gets cut in half. Be careful where you put your finger!

Business work partner
Dongeopja
동업자

Soulmate
Cheongsaengyeonbun
천생연분

Crush
Jjaksarang
짝사랑

I have a crush.
*Na **jjaksarang** hagoisseo.*
나 **짝사랑** 하고있어.

Lovers
Aein
애인

Aren't we lovers now?
*Uri ije **aein** aniya?*
우리 이제 **애인** 아니야?

Boyfriend
Namjachingu
남자친구

Do you have a boyfriend?
***Namjachingu** isseo?*
남자친구 있어?

BF
Namchin
남친

Girlfriend
Yeojachingu
여자친구

GF
Yeohchin
여친

Traitor
Baesinja
배신자

Hey, you traitor!
*Ya, i **baesinjay**a!*
야 이 **배신자**야!

Dude
Imma / Jjasik
임마 / 자식

Dude, where's my car?
***Imma**, nae cha eodinnya?*
임마, 내 차 어딨냐?

•••••Family
Gajok
가족

Family is extremely important in Korean culture. It's only recently that the divorce rate has gone up, resulting in different types of family dynamics. However, you can't just ignore the old saying, "Blood is thicker than water." Koreans put family matters before any other business. That's why in some Korean soap operas, a girl might have a baby with a guy she's just met in order to fulfill a dying grandma's wish. ("Tada! Here's your grandson, even though I hate the husband you arranged for me!") Korean society is heavy-duty with showing respect for elders. At school, a year's age difference creates a huge inequality among students—it gives the older students the right to lord it over the younger ones. They may order the "youngsters" around and even bully the poor little souls into doing anything they want. Maybe that's why Korean people can bluntly ask "How old are you?" the minute you meet them.

Mother
Eomeoni
어머니

Mom
Eomma
엄마

Father
Abeoji
아버지

Dad
Abba
아빠

SIBLING RIVALRY

It's considered rude to call your older siblings by their first names. Instead, you have to use the honorific titles "Brother" or "Sister." But it's all good for older siblings to call their younger siblings by their first names. Even if a twin sister is just two minutes younger, she still has to address her elder wombmate as "Sister."

Brother (what a girl calls her older brother)
Obba
오빠

Brother (what a boy calls his older brother)
Hyeong
형

Sister (what a girl calls her older sister)
Eonni
언니

Sister (what a boy calls his older sister)
Nuna
누나

Younger sibling
Dongsaeng
동생

Younger brother / Younger sister
Namdongsaeng / Yeodongsaeng
남동생 / 여동생

Grandmother
Halmeoni
할머니
When Grandma comes up in conversation, Koreans distinguish which side of the family (mom's or dad's) she represents. Dad's mom is called *chinhalmeoni* (친할머니), while mom's mom is referred to as *woehalmeoni* (외할머니).

Grandma
Halmae
할매
This is a more affectionate term and is typically used in rural areas.

Grandfather
Harabeoji
할아버지
When discussing Grandpa's noisy farts with friends, be sure to clarify if you're talking about your pop's pop (*chinharabeoji*; 친할아버지) or your mama's papa (*woeharabeoji*; 외할아버지).

Grandpa
Halbae
할배

Stepmother / Stepfather
Sae-eomma / Saeabba
새엄마 / 새아빠

·····Titles
Hocching
호칭

As with your siblings, it's considered disrespectful to call someone older than you by their first name. So titles like Mr., Mrs., or Miss are typically used when you're not sure of the other person's age or assume they're older than you. This can get you into trouble, though, if you end up addressing a girl with a title when she's actually younger than you. In effect, you've basically called her an old-looking hag and have ruined any chance you ever had of hooking up with her. *Congratulations.*

The title game is dangerous ground, so tread lightly. These ruinous pitfalls can be avoided if a guy calls every woman he may want to sleep with "sweet thang" (*eepeuni*; 이쁜이). Nothing can possibly go wrong by doing this!

Mr. (married)
Ajeossi
아저씨

Mr. (not married)
Chongak
총각
Used by older women.

Mrs.
Ajumma
아줌마
This term doesn't always refer to married women; it can also be used pejoratively for someone who just looks like a middle-aged housewife.

Miss
Agassi
아가씨
This is a woman who looks like she's between the age of a university student and a 30-something.

••••••Everyday people
Maeilboneun saramdeul
매일보는 사람들

Let's face it, you spend most of your life either in school or working. Yeah, maybe you get a couple of brief retirement years in the sun afterward, but by that point you're already on your way out and drinking Ensure through a straw for dinner while your caretaker wipes the dribble off your chin. So here are a few of the people you'll meet every day on your journey through life as a student or worker in Korea.

CEO / Boss
Sajangnim
사장님

My boss is a real prick.
*Uri **sajangnim**eun jinjja jaesuya.*
우리 **사장님**은 진짜 재수야.

Secretary
Biseo
비서

The secretary is sleeping her way to the top.
*Sajangi jeo **biseo**rang baramnaseo seungjinhaennabwa.*
사장이 저 **비서**랑 바람나서 승진했나봐.

Blue collar
Nodongja
노동자

That CEO looks hella blue collar!
*Jeo sajangeun dondo maneunde **nodongja** gachi eolguri sikkeomae!*
저 사장은 돈도 많은데 **노동자** 같이 얼굴이 시꺼매!

Owner
Juin
주인

Store owners are such tight-asses.
*Gagye **juindeur**eun jeongmal ssagajiya.*
가게 **주인들**은 정말 싸가지야.

Customer
Sonnim
손님

The customer is always right.
***Sonnim**eun wangiya.*
손님은 왕이야.

Government workers
Gongmuwon
공무원

Government workers can't do anything right.
***Gongmuwon** saekkideul haljulaneunge hanado eopsseo.*
공무원 새끼들 할줄아는게 하나도 없어.

Soldier
Gunin
군인
It's every Korean man's duty to serve in the military for two years.

> **Korean soldiers** think they're such hot shit.
> ***Hanguk gunindeur**eun jideuri chwegoinjool ara.*
> 한국 군인들은 지들이 최고인줄 알아.

Yankees (American soldiers)
Migun
미군
There are thousands of American military members stationed in Korea. They often stick out in a crowd with their high, tight haircuts and loud, drunken antics in bars. There has been tension between Koreans and American soldiers in the past, but now the attitude is one of general acceptance.

> All the **Yankees** are drunken meatheads.
> ***Migun** sekkideureun da sulchwihan gogideongeoriya.*
> 미군 새끼들은 다 술취한 고깃덩어리야.

••••• Student life
Hakchangsijeol
학창시절

Teacher
Sunsaengnim
선생님
Koreans highly value educated people, and it's their passion to get as much education as possible. Being a tutor is one of the most popular jobs in Korea, especially for university students. You're called "teacher" even if you're just tutoring.

> I wanna bone my **teacher.**
> *Uri **ssaem** irang neomu hagosipeo.*
> 우리 쌤이랑 너무 하고싶어.

Teach! (noun)
Ssaem!
쌤!
Warning—don't use this term with uptight teachers.

> **Yo, Teach. Let's get our learn on.**
> *Eoi, **Ssaem**, jom baewo bojago.*
> 어이, **쌤**, 좀 배워보자고.

Tutor
Gwawoe sunsaeng
과외 선생

> **My tutor is a useless shithead!**
> *Nae **gwawoe sunsaeng**eun sseulmoeopneun meongcheongiya!*
> 내 **과외선생**은 쓸모없는 멍청이야!

Student
Haksaeng
학생

Senior (in school)
Sunbae
선배
One year of age makes a huge difference in Korea. If you're a grade above your fellow students, you get to treat them like slaves!

> **The senior is using me like a slave.**
> ***Sunbae**ga na ddonggaehullyeon sikyeo.*
> **선배**가 나 똥개훈련 시켜.

Freshman
Hubae
후배
As a student at the bottom of the age totem pole, you may suffer a bit at the hands of senior bullies. But don't worry, your time will come!

> **Freshmen don't know shit.**
> ***Hubaedeur**eun jinjja amugeotdo moreunda.*
> **후배들**은 진짜 아무것도 모른다.

High school kid
Goding
고딩

Is it wrong to be attracted to high schoolers?
***Goding**hante banhamyeon andwaena?*
고딩한테 반하면 안돼나?

Middle school kid
Jungding
중딩

Who's the creeper hanging around the **middle school kids?**
*Jeo **jungding**yeopae dagaoneun byeontae nugunya?*
저 **중딩**옆에 다가오는 변태 누구냐?

Elementary school kid
Choding
초딩

Little **elementary kids** are always so snotty.
*Jwisekkimanhan **choding**deuri hangsang kkabureo.*
쥐새끼만한 **초딩**들이 항상 까불어.

••••• Characters
Gaeseongjeogin hangukin
개성적인 한국인

Unlike America's cowboy, go-it-alone mentality, Korea is very much a group society. You can almost always label anyone according to the group they seem to belong in. Koreans won't be insulted if you stereotype them based on the people they hang out with. They feel more comfortable being defined by groups than as individuals. This can be confusing or insulting to politically correct American ears, but it's a real timesaver in Korea.

Bookworm
Gongbubeollae
공부벌레

Student
Haksaeng
학생

Airhead
Golbin-nom / Golbin-nyeon
골빈놈 / 년

Wannabe gangster
Yangachi
양아치
This is an immature teenage boy who spends his parents' money on his looks and acts like a tough, wannabe gangster.

Ditz
Nallari
날라리
This is a teenager more interested in appearances than studies.

Snob
Sokmul
속물

Bean paste girl (gold digger)
Doenjangnyeo
된장녀
This term comes from someone who can't distinguish shit from bean paste! A bean paste girl is typically superficial, shallow, materialistic, and obsessed with brand-name goods. Some even use their parents' or sugar daddy's/mama's money to buy stuff to make them look glamorous. Because they're so blinded by brand names, they're ill-equipped to make judgment calls on the actual quality of items. Therefore, they'd even purchase shit if they heard it was brand-name bean paste.

The bean paste girl has yet another Gucci bag.
Jeo ***doenjangnyeo*** *tto Gucci bag deurunne.*
저 **된장녀** 또 구찌백 들었네.

Businessperson
Hoesawon
회사원

Both my parents are businesspeople who work for LG.
Uri bumonim dulda LG ***hoesawon****iya.*
우리 부모님 둘다 엘지 **회사원**이야.

Biracial
Honhyeora
혼혈아

Foreigner
Woegukin
외국인

Just learn to speak Korean already, you dumb foreigner!
Ah, hangukkmallohae meongcheonghan ***weogukin****a!*
아, 한국말로해, 멍청한 **외국인**아!

Bum
Geoji
거지

Fuck, I am sick of giving money to bums.
Sibal, ***geojideul****hante donjuneungeo jonna akkawo.*
시발, **거지들**한테 돈주는거 존나 아까워.

Loner
Wangtta
왕따

A loner may also be known as *ijime* (이지메), the word used in Japan. In Korea, a loner (usually the weakest link in a group) gets picked on by the entire class. This has become a huge social problem, with several bullied loners having committed suicide.

Police
Gyeongchal
경찰

Cops
Jjapsae
짭새

Gangsta
Jopok
조폭

> You **gangstas** think you are tough shit?
> ***Jopok*** *imyeon daya?*
> **조폭**이면 다야?

Millionaire
Buja
부자

> My **millionaire** sugar daddy buys me whatever I want!
> *Nae* ***buja*** *hogu ajeossi naega wonhaneungeo da sajo!*
> 내 **부자** 호구아저씨 내가 원하는거 다 사줘!

Broke-ass person
Gananbaengi
가난뱅이

> Quit being such a **broke-ass.**
> *Ya, don eopneun* ***gananbaengi****jit geumanhae.*
> 야, 돈없는 **가난뱅이**짓 그만해.

Unemployed person
Baeksu / Baekjo
백수 / 백조

> Hey, aren't you partying too hard for an **unemployed person?**
> *Ya,* ***baeksu****rago neomu noneungeoanya?*
> 야, **백수**라고 너무 노는거 아냐?

Genius
Cheonjae
천재

Wow, you are a genius!
Wuwa, neo jeongmal ***cheonjae****ya!*
우와, 너 정말 **천재**야!

Princess
Gongju
공주

It's nice to be called a princess by your parents when you are five, but if you're still "Princess" when you're a teenager, you've got to admit that you're a conceited bitch.

You have a serious princess syndrome!
Neo simhan ***gongjubyeong****iya!*
너 심한 **공주병**이야!

Young girls should be the most darling princesses to their parents, but if you act like one, it's considered being delusional—hence "princess syndrome."

Prince
Wangja
왕자

On the flip side, a *wangja* is a conceited Korean who, in his own mind, is a perfect prince that all the girls want. Wait, don't all guys think that?

Average Joe
Pyeongbeomhan saram
평범한 사람

Don't try to stand out; being an average Joe is best.
Neomu twijimara, ***pyeongbeomhan****ge choegoya.*
너무 튀지마라, **평범한**게 최고야.

Jesus freak
Yesujaengi
예수쟁이

Jesus freaks think they are married to God.
Haneunnimgwa gyeolhonhan michin ***yesujaengideul****.*
하는님과 결혼한 미친 **예수쟁이들**.

CHAPTER 3

PARTY KOREAN

HANGUKAESUH NOLTTAE HANEUNMAL

한국에서 놀때 하는말

•••••Let's party!

Uri nolja!

우리 놀자!

When it comes to partying, Koreans are the Irish of Asia. They get all red-faced when they get drunk, which is often. Unlike in the States, though, Koreans don't just park themselves at one bar. They won't stop until they've gone to at least four places to drink *soju*, beer, *makgeolli* (Korean rice drink), wine, and hard liquor. In fact, partying is such an integral part of Korean culture that you can't say you've truly experienced Korea until you've gotten drunk as shit off cheap *soju*, performed bad karaoke, and then watched yourself on YouTube (thanks to your thoughtful friends) singing and dancing to Korean songs you've never heard before.

Put it in the calendar!
Kelbak
캘박

Hey, it's decided. **Put it in the calendar!**
*Ya, iguh **kelbak** heh*
야 이거 **캘박**해.

A cafe with a great vibe.
Bunjoka
분조카

Let's go to the **cafe** in Hongdae that has **great vibes.**
*Hongdae-eh **bunjoka** gaja.*
홍대에 **분조카** 가자.

Awesome. Sounds good.
King ah
킹아.

Are you up for...
Junbi dwaennya...
준비 됐냐...

partying?
nol junbi dwaennya?
놀 준비 됐냐?

drinking?
sul masil junbi dwaennya?
술 마실 준비 됐냐?

going out?
nagal junbi dwaennya?
나갈 준비 됐냐?

getting wasted?
jugeul junbi dwaennya?
죽을 준비 됐냐?
Literally, "Are you ready to die?" Koreans don't want to stop drinking until they black out!

a drink?
hanjan hal junbi dwaennya?
한잔 할 준비 됐냐?

Bottoms up!
Won syat!
원샷!
Literally "one shot," alluding to the fact that you don't get to sip *soju* in Korea. You drink all of it at once—or your Korean drinking buddies will push you until you learn how to do so. So learn quick!

First round / Second round / Third round
Ilcha / icha / samcha
일차 / 이차 / 삼차
In the US, the first, second, and third rounds may be at the same bar, but in Korea each round takes place in a different drinking establishment. As they say in Korea, the first is to eat and drink, the second is to sing and drink more, and the third is to drink even more.

Do you have a plan?
Mo ***halggeo*** *eopnya?*
뭐 **할거** 없냐?

Where are you headed?
Eodiga?
어디가?

Let's have a drink.
Sul *hanjan haja.*
술 한잔 하자.

Let's go for **round 2.**
*Uri **icha** gaja!*
우리 **이차** 가자!

Let's drink **till the end!**
*Uri hanbeon **kkeukkaji** gaboja!*
우리 한번 **끝까지** 가보자!

Let's drink **till we die!**
*Uri hanbeon **jugeo**boja.*
우리 한번 **죽어**보자.

Do you know any **hot spots?**
***Mul joeun got** ara?*
물 좋은 곳 알아?

Let's **stay up all night!**
*Uri **bamsaeja**!*
우리 **밤새자**!

Let's drink just **one more bottle**!
*Uri ttak **hanbyeongman deo** haja!*
우리 딱 **한병만 더** 하자!

Let's play **till the sunrise!**
***Hae tteul ttaekkaji** nolja!*
해 뜰 때까지 놀자!

Cheers!
Geonbae!
건배~

> **Cheers** to a long and drunken night!
> ***Geonbae**! Uri jugeoboja!*
> **건배**! 우리 죽어보자!

Cin cin!
Jjan!
짠!

Cin cin to a bottomless glass!
***Jjan** haja!*
짠 하자!

Let's raise a glass.
Jan deulja.
잔 들자.

......Where Koreans get down
Nolgeori
놀거리

Koreans don't just go on bar crawls. Oh no, they're far more determined about their drunken debauchery than that. After dinner (which itself will feature copious amounts of drinking) on a typical Korean night out, you'll hit up a plethora of bars for a spectacular evening of drunken imbibing before moving onward to a *noraebang*, or karaoke house—where you'll get even more plastered while performing slurred renditions of '80s pop hits. If you're still on your feet after that, you might cap things off at a club for yet more drinking or—if you need to sober up—at the *jimjilbang*, a 24-hour sauna where you can leech all that delicious poison out of your body.

Bar
Suljip
술집
In areas such as Hongdae, a district of Seoul surrounding an artsy university, there are strips of bars catering to your every mood—fusion bars, traditional Korean bars, Westernized bars, Japanese bars, and karaoke bars. If you don't like the joint you've meandered into, just pick up and move on to the next!

Karaoke house
Noraebang
노래방

Your voice might suck, but honestly, in Korea nobody gives a shit. Karaoke is something of a Korean national pastime, and it's always done in private rooms where you can butcher Journey songs with only your friends around to make fun of you. And it only costs about $20–$30 an hour to rent a room!

You sing well.
***Norae** jom hane.*
노래 좀 하네.

Club
Club
클럽
Guys and girls of ages 18 to 30 go to a club to dance their asses off. (Well, dancing your ass off is something you can do at home in front of your mirror—I don't want to see any jiggly asses.) If you are looking for a hot one-night stand with a drunken friend you won't remember the next day, or if you're just too drunk to care, there are great clubs all over. Since techtonic is so hot in Korea, all the clubs play similar music. In Seoul, the Hongdae area is filled with tons of options, but Itaewon's the place to go if you're looking for Korean girls ready to throw themselves at handsome foreigners. It's also the place where all the foreigners hang out. Gangnam's another good place to check out; it's also home to two well-known hip-hop clubs, Harlem and NB.

Are there any hot girls at the club?
***Clube** mul joa?*
클럽에 물 좋아?

ID check / Dress code check
Mul gwalli
물관리
Bouncers in Korea do ID checks and, more importantly, enforce a dress code. So you'd better look bangin' if you want to get in!

Nightclub
Night
나이트
The difference between nightclubs and clubs is a fat wallet. At clubs, guys can use charm and dance skills to hook up. But if men want to expend less energy on the game and they have

some Benjamins to throw around, they head to the nightclubs, typically referred to as "night." All the girls are hotties who get free admission and drinks because, well, they're hotties. Guys shell out a ridiculously high cover to enter and then also get to pay for all the drinks inside. But all that green being thrown around means you get to stare at, talk to, and/or dance with the pretty thangs all you want. You can even ask a waiter to bring your favorite girl to your table—without fear of a "no way, Jose."

FAMOUS DISTRICTS IN SEOUL

YU MYEONGHAN GOT

유명한 곳

Hongdae

홍대

The Hongdae district is known for its clubs and for creative types selling homemade jewelry on the street (read: Korean hippies). It's kinda like Korea's version of Berkeley, but with more clubs and bars. (Can you imagine that?)

Apgujeong

압구정

Home to many celebrities, Apgujeong is the Beverly Hills of Korea. It's great if you like shopping centers and overpriced cafés.

Myeongdong

명동

This famous area features huge malls with cheap goods as well as some street shops that are great for exploring. It's where most Japanese tourists come to buy stuff, so if you're a shopper you need to check it out. But if you're looking for brand names and high quality, you're in the wrong place—Koreans are known for producing brand imitations, and this venue showcases many such knockoffs.

Insadong

인사동

Insadong features traditional Korean shopping centers where you can buy souvenirs and other touristy crap for your family and friends. There are also lots of old-fashioned teahouses where you can experience authentic Korean tea if you need somewhere to bring your parents or someone you're trying to impress.

Yeouido

여의도
Seoul's business and administrative center, Yeouido has plentiful public parks that attract weekend bicyclists and bladers. And the views of the country's famous Han River are spectacular.

Olympic Park
Olympic gongwon
올림픽 공원
The stadium and surrounding park were built for the 1988 Summer Olympics. On weekends, families and friends come here to picnic and bike.

North Gate / East Gate
Namdaemun / Dongdaemun
남대문 / 동대문
These gates mark Seoul's original borders. Now there are 24-hour shopping districts here—isn't modernization great?

Booking
Booking
부킹
This nightclub practice involves tipping waiters who will then escort women to men's tables, where chicks imbibe expensive drinks in exchange for their company. The crazy thing is that even though the babes know what's going on, the chosen women still put up a show of resistance—you know, for modesty's sake. While a female might "book" a guy, it's pretty rare (she'd probably be considered a ho, and therefore undesirable). Of course, men do try to get the women drunk enough to leave the club with them for more intimate places. Wink, wink!

Club promoter
Bbikki
삐끼
Club promoters often approach you on the street with special offers or promotions.

Playground
Noriteo
놀이터

There are playgrounds in nearly every apartment complex in Korea, and they often turn into gathering places for teens to get together and drink at night.

Rooftop
Oksang
옥상
Seoul is covered with tall apartment buildings, most of them over 25 stories tall. It's fun to sneak up to the rooftop of a building and party like a rock star above the city.

Sauna
Jjimjilbang
찜질방
Korean saunas, with partitioned bathhouses for men and women, are open 24/7. Normally used for family nights, saunas have different common areas to choose from. One room may have PCs or DVDs, while another may offer manicures or massages. You can even pick up a snack or sleep here—if you're too drunk and broke to catch a cab home. It's only about $10 a night, and you'll even look pretty presentable the next day.

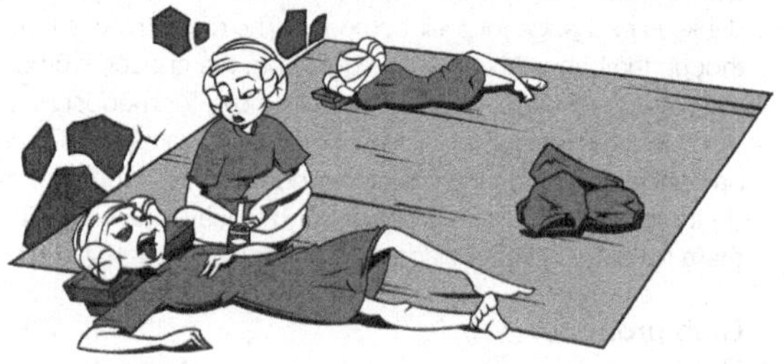

Playroom
Noribang
놀이방
Teenagers rent these common rooms at motels; each comes complete with a shower, a bed, and a PlayStation. It's a great place to meet up and chill. You can even throw a fabulous party here—just add balloons, ribbon, dresses—and, of course, booze.

PC café
PC bang
피씨방
PC cafés provide some of the fastest internet service in the world. Kids love to come here to play video games. You can even catch some gamers skipping school to play online games here. Fan of WoW? Check out the PC cafés.

Manga café
Manhwabang
만화방
These are like Korean libraries for people who like to dick off reading magazines and Manga comics instead of studying. You can smoke and eat here, too.

Video room
Bidiobang
비디오방
These rooms, furnished with a couch and a TV, are where underage students go—supposedly to watch movies, but really to end up having sex.

Wine bar
Wainba
와인바
Sophisticated white-collar people (i.e., pretentious jerks) like to eat at elegant wine bars. Take your girlfriend to a glamorous wine bar with eye-popping high prices, and she just might give you what you've been waiting for.

Hof
Hopeu
호프
The German word *Hof* originally means "court" or "yard," and in the context of beer, it's short for *Bierhof* (beer garden or beer hall). During the 1970s and 1980s in Korea, Western-style beer bars started popping up, and *Hof* was adopted from German beer culture, especially inspired by places like Hofbräuhaus in Munich—a famous beer hall.

Trailer bar
Pojangmacha
포장마차
Trailers are typically outdoor tents on wheels that offer street food such as chicken feet, with *soju* as a beverage. These places are usually open until 4 or 5 in the morning, and they're where Koreans without a lot of money go to get drunk and talk to friends.

•••••Totally wasted
Sul chwiham
술 취함

Koreans don't fuck around when it comes to getting their drink on. Getting plastered is an art in Korea, and certain customs must be followed. For instance, it's traditional that someone else at the table pours your drink (and you theirs)—it's a gesture of respect and friendship. If you do it yourself, you're rejecting this. So be sure to keep a steady supply of friends on hand, because unless you're a pussy lightweight, you're gonna need a lot of drinks poured your way.

Holy shit, I'm...
Ssibal, na...
씨발, 나...

a little tipsy.
*jom **eojireowo**.*
좀 어지러워.

smashed.
gondeurae mandeurae.
곤드래 만드래.

trashed.
manchwihessuh.
만취했어.

plastered.
kkoratda.
꼴았다.

hammered.
kkwaladwaetda.
꽐라됐다.

I am **buzzed!**
Na ***chwihaneungeo*** *gata!*
나 **취하는거** 같아!

Men aren't supposed to use the word "drunk" in Korea. So even if you're drunk, just act like everything is fine and pretend you can hold your liquor.

I **blacked out** last night.
Na eoje ***pileum kkeunkkyeosseosseo.***
나 어제 **필름 끊겼었어.**

I am about to **throw up.**
Na ***ssollyeo.***
나 **쏠려.**

I'm gonna **hurl.**
Na ***ssonneunda.***
나 **쏟는다.**

I have to **vomit.**
Na ***to*** *haeyahae.*
나 **토**해야해.

I just **blew chunks** everywhere.
Na jigeum ***bburyeosseo.***
나 지금 **뿌렸어.**

You are **slurring.**
Nu ***hyeo kkoinda.***
너 **혀 꼬인다.**

•••••Booze

Sul

술

In Korea, you never refuse a drink poured by an elder (you know, that whole age-hierarchy thing). So if you're partying with older friends, you may be in for a rough night. Hopefully they'll take pity on you and stop pouring you drinks before you end up taking a transvestite to a love motel. But if they don't, at least you'll have a funny story to tell the next day. That, and lots of shame.

Gimme a ...
... juseyo.
... 주세요.

soju.
Soju
소주

The ubiquitous *soju*, traditionally made from rice, is Korea's answer to vodka. It's cheap and will get you fucked up. A lot of celebrities shell out big money for special *soju* brands, but they're all basically watered-down versions of American vodka.

Order me another yogurt *soju*—I haven't passed out yet.
Ya, yogurutu soju hanbyung duh cikyuh! Na a-jig jungsin maljjanghae.
야, 요구르트 소주 한병 더 시켜! 나 아직 정신 말짱해.

unfiltered rice wine.
Makgeolli / Takju
막걸리 / 탁주

A cloudy concoction that's historically been a farmer's drink, this Korean sake has recently become en vogue with the younger generation. It's cheap, sweet, and best served with *buchimgae*, Korean pancakes.

beer.
Maekju
맥주
Popular Korean beers include Hite and OB. Drink your beer cold with Korean fried chicken, and you're in business!

liquor.
Yangju.
양주
This term is used to describe any drink coming from the West—wine, brandy, whiskey, vodka, etc.

Korean sake.
Jeongjong
정종

Korean medicine drink.
Baekseju
백세주
Baekseju is a brand of *soju* made for girls who can't tolerate the smell and taste of "regular" *soju*. This sweet drink, flavored with ginseng, is actually good for you if you limit your drinking to a bottle or less (like that ever happens).

> **Eunjug Kim is such a lightweight that she only drinks Korean medicine drink.**
> *Kim Eun-jung eun neomu swipge chwihanda. **Baekseju**man masine.*
> 김은정은 너무 쉽게 취한다. **백세주**만 마시네.

raspberry drink.
Bokbunja
복분자
This tends to be popular with the ladies because of its sweetness. It's also supposedly viagra-in-a-bottle for guys (but if you drink too much of it, you'll be too shit-faced to get it up, so take your chances).

·····Drinking games

Sul game

술 게임

These games are extremely popular in Korea. They're like beer pong, but done at a bar and usually played sitting down.

The Game of Death

Deo game ob desseu

더 게임어브 데트

A group will often start out with this game to get each other drunk quickly. It's pretty much a no-brainer—you chant "the game of death" and point at someone you'd like to see drunk. The one with the most fingers pointed at them has to drink. It's crude but effective at getting everyone fucked up.

Titanic (aka, Sake Bomb)

Titanic

타이타닉

This is like a sake bomb, with *soju* instead of sake. But you don't just make a soju bomb (*poktanju*) and down it—all the drinkers participate in creating the Titanic. First you pour half a glass of beer. Then you set an empty soju glass in the glass of beer. People take turns pouring as much soju as they want into the beer glass. Whoever sinks the soju glass has to drink the whole thing. Bottom's up!

King Game

King game

킹 게임

Gather chopsticks (yes, Koreans eat with chopsticks, so you'd have them) equal to the number of participants (e.g., five players = five chopsticks). Put the letter "K" (for "King") on one chopstick and then number the remaining chopsticks, starting with 1. Each person then picks a chopstick. The person with the K chopstick can make the others do whatever he or she wants.

For example, the king can make numbers 1 and 4 kiss each other. If you are both dudes, well, enjoy the hot breath.

Black Knight
Heukgisa
흑기사
This is when a woman finds a man to take a shot for her while playing a drinking game. The girl normally has to do a favor for him afterward (sexual or otherwise).

Black Rose
Heukjangmi
흑장미
The exact opposite of the Black Knight, this is when a man asks a woman to take a shot for him in a drinking game. But if she refuses, he has to take double shots.

3, 6, 9
Sam yuk gu
삼육구
Everyone sits at a table and goes around counting up from 1. You clap on every number that contains 3, 6, and 9. If you fail to clap or say your number, you have to chug.

APT
ahpateu
아파트
In 2024, Rosé and Bruno Mars' hit single "APT" introduced the world to this popular Korean drinking game. You chant, "ahpateu, ahpateu" (which means "apartment") with a circle of friends, then everyone stacks their hands into a pile. Someone shouts out a random number to designate a "floor" of the apartment, and you and your friends begin stacking one hand on top of the others, one by one, building a tower until someone lands on the chosen floor number and has to take a shot!

The Baskin Robbins 31
Baskin Robbins Sseotiwon
베스킨 로빈스 써리원
Someone starts counting from 1, and the next person continues counting, in order, saying one to three numbers per turn. So if you begin by saying "1," the next player can say "2," "2, 3" or "2, 3, 4." The person who gets to 31 has to drink.

••••••Taking it easy today

Oneureun swillae

오늘은 쉴래

Your liver can only take so much abuse before it goes into revolt. So when you've had enough and can't take another night of hard living at the *noraebang*, try out some of these phrases on your new friends—and prepare yourself to be called several iterations of the word "pussy."

I am dying from a **hangover.**
Sukchi *ttaemune jugeulkkeo gata.*
숙취 때문에 죽을꺼 같아.

I'm **still drunk** from last night.
Eoje masin sule ajikdo ***chwihesseo.***
어제 마신 술에 **아직도 취했어.**

I think I have **cirrhosis.**
Na ***ganyeom*** *inneungeo gata.*
나 **간염**있는것 같아.

It's too much, **count me out.**
Oneureun ***bbaejo,*** *na himdeureo.*
오늘은 **빼줘**, 나 힘들어.

Pass.
Oneureun ***pass.***
오늘은 **패스**.

See you **next time.**
Da-eume *boja.*
다음에 보자.

I need to go home **early.**
Na jibe ***iljjik*** *gabwaya dwae.*
나 집에 **일찍** 가봐야 돼.

My curfew is 10.
***Tongeumi** yeolsiya.*
통금이 10시야.

I'm just gonna chill tonight.
*Nan oneul geunyang **swillae**.*
난 오늘 그냥 **쉴래**.

I'm a bed-wetting little girl and **I can't handle my liquor.**
***Na** aegiraseo **sul mot masyeo**.*
나 애기라서 **술 못 마셔**.

......Drugs

Mayak

마약

Unlike America, where there's a pill for everything, Korean culture isn't big on drugs, recreational or otherwise. Even over-the-counter medications such as pain relievers aren't widely used. That's not to say that nobody does drugs in Korea. It's just not a mainstream thing that you hear talked about that much.

Have you ever tried **drugs?**
*Neo **mayak** haebwasseo?*
너 **마약** 해봤어?

Weed
Daemacho
대마초

Although weed is generally a pretty harmless drug and treated as such in most of the world, in Korea it falls into the same category as hard drugs such as cocaine and heroin—and the cops treat them all the same. That's right, a measly little joint could add up to serious jail time—so toke at your own risk.

Where can I get some weed?
***Daemacho** eodiseo guhalsu isseo?*
대마초 어디서 구할수 있어?

Pot
Tteol
떡

Pothead
Tteoljaengi
떡쟁이
Most hard drugs get into the country through foreigners or Korean students who study abroad, so college parties would likely be your best bet if you're looking for a hookup to drugs.

Heroin
Heroin
헤로인

Horse (heroin)
Hirobbong
히로뽕

Why is she acting like she's on the horse?
*Jeonyeon wae **hirobbong** han haengdongeul hanya?*
저년 왜 **히로뽕** 한 행동을 하냐?

CIGARETTES

DAMBAE

담배

Cigarettes are very popular in Korea. That's not surprising, since every other drug is so hard to get. And just as in the US, lots of kids are vaping nowadays.

E-cigarette
Jundam
전담

Can you recommend a flavor of **e-cigarette**?
Jeondam aeksang chucheonhae juseyo?
전담 액상 추천해 주세요?

Filter
Aeksang
액상

Vaping
Be i ping
베이핑

Can I bum a cig?
Dambae handae billil soo itseulkkayo?
담배 한대 빌릴 수 있을까요?

Do you have a light?
Laita isseuseyo?
라이터 있으세요?

Coke
Cokein
코케인

Fentanyl
Pentanil
펜타닐

Ecstasy
Exteossi
엑스터시
You can get this at a lot of clubs in urban areas if you know the right person.

Addiction
Jungdok
중독

Addict
Jungdokja
중독자

> **Can you be addicted to weed?**
> *Daemachoe **jungdok** dwelsu isseo?*
> 대마초에 **중독**될 수 있어?

Crackhead
Matgannom / Matgannyeon
맛간놈 / 맛간년

> **That girl ain't nothing but a crackhead.**
> *Jeonyeon wanjeon **matgannyeon**ine.*
> 저년 완전 **맛간년**이네.

Junky
Mayakjaengi / Yakjaengi
마약쟁이 / 약쟁이

> **Some junky just offered to suck my dick for crack.**
> *Eotteon **yakjaengi**ga jigeum mayak jumyeon oral haejugetde.*
> 어떤 **약쟁이**가 지금 마약 주면 오랄 해주겠데.

Korean Krazy Glue
Bbondeu
본드

Since illegal substances are hard to obtain, some Korean high school kids love to get high off of everyday items that you can get from hardware stores, such as Krazy Glue and butane gas.

> **Do you want to get high with Krazy Glue?**
> *Bbondeu bbalgo **bbyong galkka**?*
> 본드빨고 **뽕 갈까**?

> **I huffed some glue.**
> *Bbondeu **bbarasseo.***
> 본드 **빨았어**.

Butane gas
Butan gas
부탄가스

> **I went crazy after huffing butane gas.**
> *Butan gas **masigo** dorasseo.*
> 부탄가스 **마시고** 돌았어.

CHAPTER 4

POPPY KOREAN

HANGOOK ENTERTAINMENT

한국 엔터테인먼트

As with many Asian countries, Korea has been heavily influenced by American pop culture. Fast food chains such as McDonald's are ubiquitous, and Western-style fashion is all the rage. But Korean culture is made up of more than just Western rip-offs. In the past few years, exports of Korean pop culture have surged, including TV dramas, music, and movies. Dubbed the "Korean Wave," this cultural phenomenon has helped raise Korea's profile and boost tourism.

••••••Music

Eumak

음악

Let's listen to some...

...deutja.

...듣자.

Let's bump some...

...teulja.

... 틀자.

I wanna hear some...
Na ... deutgo sipeo.
나 ... 듣고 싶어.

K-pop.
pop
팝
You might want to dismiss Korean popular music as foreign music, but you can't. K-pop is taking over the world! With BTS and Blackpink dominating music charts in the US and on world tours, you'll wanna learn some K-pop dance moves!

ballad.
ballad
발라드
Seung-hoon Shin (신승훈) is the Korean king of ballads. (For some reason, there aren't many female balladeers in Korea.) Most ballads become popularized when they are the theme songs for TV shows.

rock.
rock
락
Rock is a somewhat strange genre to Koreans—they think rock singers are dark, weird people. But rockers need not despair! Do-hyun Yoon and a group called Boohwal (부활), meaning "rebirth," fill this small niche.

indie.
indie
인디
You can find a lot of indie rock musicians in the Hongdae district of Seoul.

rap.
rap
랩
A favorite rap group is Drunken Tiger. Their lyrics are genius.

reggae.
reggae
레게
Gun-mo Kim (김건모) is a self-proclaimed Korean reggae artist. He may not be great, but he's the best we've got.

••••••K-pop

pop
팝

Bias
Che-ae
최애
Fans of K-pop groups often have a favorite member of the group, called a bias. But if you start liking another member more than your original bias, that member becomes your bias-wrecker.

Who's your BTS bias?
Nueu BTS che-ae-ga noogooya?
너의 BTS 최애가 누구야?

Bias-wrecker
Cha-ae
차애

She's my bias-wrecker!
Gye nae cha-ae-ya!
걔 내 차애야!

Photo cards
Po-ka
포카

Limited-edition photo card
Mi-gong-po
미공포

Did you get the limited photo card?
Mi-gong-po satsuh?
미공포 샀어?

Stan
Deok-jil
덕질

I stan BTS.
Na BTS deokjil hajanna.
나 BTS 덕질하잖아.

Die-hard fan
Gwang pan
광팬

I'm a die-hard fan of Blackpink.
Na Blackpink gwangpaniya.
나 블랙핑크 광팬이야.

Starting to stan a K-pop artist.
Ipdeok
입덕

I started stanning the group after I heard their song.
Nore deuego ipdeok haejjana.
노래 듣고 입덕 했잖아.

•••••K-drama

Drama

드라마

Let's watch a...

...boja

... 보자

soap opera.

drama

드라마

Well known for love triangles and tragic storylines, Korean dramas (akin to American soap operas) are extremely popular throughout Asia and the whole world. Korean television shows have gotten so popular that tons of Japanese tourists come to Korea to visit the areas where scenes were filmed.

series.

drama

드라마

The series is hot these days.

Geu drama yozeum umchung hottae.

그 드라마 요즘 엄청 핫해.

Lead actor

Namjoo

남주

The male lead actor is super hot.

Namjoo wanjeon jal sangyussuh.

남주 완전 잘 생겼어.

Lead actress

Yeojoo

여주

Isn't the lead actress fugly?

Yeojooga motsaengjiji anassuh?

여주가 못생기지 않았어?

Soap opera
Makjang drama
막장드라마

That's totally over the top.
Geuguh wanjeon makjangyiya.
그거 완전 막장이야.

Binge-watching
Jeongjoohang
정주행

I'm binge-watching a classic Korean drama series.
Na yozeum yetnal drama da jeongjoohang joongyiya.
나 요즘 옛날 드라마 다 정주행중이야.

Web drama
Web drama
웹드라마

I watch web dramas these days.
Nan yozeum web drama bwa.
난 요즘 웹드라마 봐.

•••••Netflix
Netpeulliksеu
넷플릭스

Netflix has been actively producing and adding Korean series (K-dramas) to its platform, many of which have gained immense popularity worldwide.

Squid Game
O-jing-eoh game
오징어게임
This survival drama series became a global phenomenon on Netflix, exploring dark themes through a deadly competition.

Kingdom
Kingdom
킹덤
This historical horror-thriller series is set in the Joseon era of Korean history, when a mysterious plague turns people into flesh-eating zombies. It follows a crown prince's quest to uncover the truth behind the epidemic and to save his kingdom.

CARTOONS
MANHWA
만화

Anime
Ilbon manhwa yeonghwa
일본만화영화
Japanese anime is very popular in Korea. *Sailor Moon*, *Pokémon*, *Dragon Ball*, and other classics were airing here way before they were imported to America. If you're an anime fan, you'll find a lot of friends in Korea. Let your geek flag fly!

Animation (usually referring to Korean anime)
Manhwa yeonghwa
만화영화
Protagonists in Korean animations are more human than the fantastical sci-fi characters with magical powers coming out of Japan. Some of the most famous shows are *Dooyi* (둘리), the story of a time-traveling baby dinosaur; *Hani* (하니), the tale of an orphan girl who becomes a runner; and *Dokgotak* (독고탁), the story of a poor young boy who becomes a famous baseball player.

Manga
Manhwachaek
만화책
Being a comic book nerd may not get you laid in the US, but you don't need to be shy about reading *manhwachaek* in Korea. It's an accepted part of pop culture, and people talk about comic book characters as if they're family members. A lot of *manhwachaek* stories get reproduced as TV shows and movies.

......Movies

Hanguk yeonghwa

한국영화

Korean movies have gained popularity throughout Asia and the US, and Hollywood has even adapted several Korean movies into American films (e.g., *The Lake House*, starring Keanu Reeves and Sandra Bullock). Of course, watching the originals is recommended! Even with subtitles, you'll get the morals behind the stories rather than just seeing American glitz and big-name actors.

Parasite

Gisengchoong

기생충

Parasite is a 2019 South Korean film directed by Bong Joon-ho. It follows the Kim family, who through deception exploit their way into the lives of the wealthy Park family. The film explores themes of class inequality and privilege with dark humor and a gripping storyline, culminating in a shocking climax. *Parasite* received widespread acclaim, winning the Palme d'Or at Cannes and four Oscars, including Best Picture, for its compelling narrative and stellar performances.

Oldboy

Oldeu boy

올드보이

Oldboy is a 2003 South Korean film directed by Park Chan-wook. Part of his Vengeance Trilogy, it follows Oh Dae-su, who is mysteriously imprisoned for 15 years and seeks revenge upon his release, uncovering dark truths along the way. Known for its intense storyline and iconic cinematography, *Oldboy* has left a lasting impact on global cinema.

•••••Computer / Internet

Computer / Internet

컴퓨터 / 인터넷

Korea is at the forefront of adopting and implementing new technology. Even the high-speed internet that you see in the US is too slow for Koreans—their entire infrastructure has been upgraded to an ultra-ultra-fast fiber-optic connection that's not available to all Americans. And to further put Americans to shame, Koreans are rumored to be the best hackers around.

YouTube Korea

Korean YouTube is a vibrant platform with a diverse range of content catering to both domestic and international audiences. Overall, Korean YouTube reflects the country's diverse interests, cultural richness, and technological innovation, making it a dynamic platform for reaching global audiences and sharing Korean culture with the world.

Online videos
Dongyeongsang
동영상

Naver.com
Neibuh
네이버
Naver is the Korean search engine equivalent of Google and Yahoo.

> **Who needs books when you have Naver?**
> ***Neibuhga*** *itneunde chaegi wae piryohae?*
> **네이버가** 있는데 책이 왜 필요해?

My computer is down.
Nae ***computer*** *downdwaesseo.*
내 **컴퓨터** 다운됐어.

I've never used a Mac before.
Na ***mac*** *hanbeondo sseobonjeok upsseo.*
나 **맥** 한번도 써본적 없어.
Macs actually aren't popular in Korea.

I saw an iPod yesterday, and it was beautiful.
*Eojae **iPod** bwatneunde ibbeudeora.*
어제 **아이팟** 봤는데 이쁘더라.

INSTANT MESSAGING

CHATTING HALTTAE HANEU NMAL

체팅할때 하는말

@
Golbaengi
골뱅이

Emoticon
이모티콘

OTL / OZL
오티엘 / 오지엘
This emoticon is used when you're feeling down and self-deprecating. It's a full-body profile of a human figure down on its hands and knees. "O" is the head, "T" is the upper torso and hands, and "L" is the shape of the legs. With "OZL," the "Z" indicates the figure down on the forearms instead.

Haha
hehe
ㅎㅎ
keke
ㅋㅋ

=)
^.^
=0
^o^
Y-Y
ㅜ.ㅜ / ㅠ.ㅠ

•••••Cell phone
Handphone
핸드폰

Korea leads the world in cell phone technology. Korean companies are constantly updating their models, and it's considered a status symbol in Korea to have the most up-to-date phone.

iPhone
A-I-pon
아이폰

Samsung phone
Samsung pon
삼성폰

Video phone chat
Young tong
영통

Text message
Munjja
문자

KakaoTalk
Katok
카톡
This is the main messenger app that Koreans use. You'd better download it if you want to talk to Koreans!

•••••Horror
Gongpo
공포

Koreans love horror stories—and they're especially popular in the summer, when Koreans watch tons of scary TV shows and movies (in air-conditioned comfort) to help them forget about the sweltering weather.

Scary story
Museowun yaegi
무서운 얘기

Tell me a ghost story.
Gwisinyaegi haejwo.
귀신얘기 해줘.

It's scary.
Museopda.
무섭다.

Scary school stories
Hakgyo gwoedam
학교 괴담
Korean people love scary stories about students who die in school. It's one of the more animated topics of conversation that students discuss when hanging out after school.

Ghost
Gwisin
귀신

Virgin ghost
Cheonyeo gwisin
처녀귀신
Most Korean scary stories include ghosts, but odds are the ghost is a virgin who meets an unfortunate death before marriage. This keeps her coming back to the real world to avenge her wrongful death. Another popular ghost character is called *dalgyal gwisin* (달걀귀신), meaning "egg ghost" because it lacks a face.

Exorcist
Twoemasa
퇴마사

Chinese zombie
Gangssi
강시
The Chinese zombie is prevalent in Korean movies and comics. Normally zombies can be defeated by a *bujeok* (부적), or paper charm. If only all threats were that simple to deal with!

Fortune teller
Jeomjaengi
점쟁이
Korean fortune tellers don't use crystal balls to see your future. Instead, they ask for names and birthdays in order to tell peoples' fortunes.

> **Tell me my fortune.**
> *Jeom bwajuseyo.*
> 점 봐주세요.

Shaman
Mudang
무당
The Korean shaman is typically summoned to comfort ghosts.

Korean monster
Dokkaebi
도깨비
Similar to the Japanese *oni*, the *dokkaebi* is a gargoyle-looking character that has its own magic bat, called *dokkaebi bangmangi* (도깨비 방망이). It's known for its mischievous behavior meant to scare bad people.

Death god
Jeoseungsaja
저승사자
This character wears a black outfit with a traditional Korean hat (*gat*; 갓) made of hairs from horse tails. He comes to drag you to the underworld.

••••••Fashion

Pashion

패션

Korean fashion trends are lifted directly from American pop culture and Korean TV shows. What popular actors and actresses are wearing instantly becomes trendy.

Sell-out celebrity
Wanpannyeo / nam
완판녀 / 남
These celebrities cash in on their fame by shamelessly wearing their endorsement products. And it works—the stuff sells out in stores!

Check out the trendy hair on that K-pop dude!
Jeo hanguk yeonaein yuhaenghan meori style bwa!
저 한국 연애인 유행한 머리 스타일 봐!

I love your retro look.
Neo bokgopung gwaenchanta.
너 복고풍 괜찮다.

White-washed jeans are so vintage.
Mul bbajin cheongbajineun bintiji lookiya.
물 빠진 청바지는 빈티지 룩이야.

I love Lil Weezy's hip-hop swag.
Nan Lil Weezy hip-hop style-i joteora.
난 리를 위지 힙합 스타일이 좋더라.

The power tie is what really makes the business style.
Nektaireul maeya jeongjang style-iya.
넥타이를 매야 정장 스타일이야.
You can forget about casual Fridays in Korea—all businessmen wear suits. Period.

Korean chicks are always so trendy.
Hanguk yeojadeureun eonjena trendyhae.
한국 여자들은 언제나 트랜디해.

The mainstream look is soooo boring.
Yuhaenghan lookeun neomu jigyeowo.
유행한 룩은 너무 지겨워.

Your mom has awesome style.
Neone eommaneun sikhae.
너네 엄마는 시크해.

Lookin' stylish!
Meotjaengine!
멋쟁이네!

Damn, Lady Gaga is looking tacky!
Lady Gaga chontinanda.
레이디 가가 촌티난다.

CHAPTER 5

BODY KOREAN

HANGUKESEO WOEMOE GWANHAE YAEGIHANEUN MAL

한국에서 외모에 관해 얘기하는 말

•••••The Korean ideal

Hanguk minam mi-in

한국 미남 미인

Koreans are increasingly adopting Western ideals of beauty. They want to be taller and skinnier, possess a higher and pointier nose, and have whiter skin. In fact, Westerners are big hits in Korea. So if you're striking out in the good ol' U.S. of A. because you're not "exotic looking," you might be a home run in Korea. But if you're hoping to find a Korean who will love you for your inner beauty, wake up. Koreans are very superficial—so superficial, in fact, that the nation ranks number one per capita in plastic surgery.

Koreans want to look more Western. Korean men want to look like Michelangelo's statue of David, and women want to be Venus. So naturally, Koreans want different eyes, noses, mouths, and ears than what they already have.

Facial features
Imokgubi
이목구비

He has striking features.
Geueui eolgureun ***imokgubiga ttoryeothae.***
그의 얼굴은 **이목구비가 또렷해.**

He / She is...
Geuneun / Geunyeoneun...
그는... / 그녀는...

cute.
gwiyeopda.
귀엽다.

pretty.
Yaebbeuda.
예쁘다.

beautiful.
areumdapda.
아름답다.

sexy.
sseksihada.
섹시하다.

good looking. (for men)
minamida.
미남이다.

good looking. (for women)
minyeoida.
미녀이다.

popular.
ingiga jota.
인기가 좋다.

skinny.
mallatda.
말랐다.

tall.
kigakeuda.
키가크다.

ripped. (too muscular)
urakburak hada.
우락부락 하다.
This has a negative connotation in Korean.

buff.
tantanhada.
탄탄하다.

voluptuous.
jjukjjuk bbangbbang hada.
쭉쭉빵빵 하다.

handsome.
jal saengyeotda.
잘 생겼다.

metrosexual.
kkonminam i da.
꽃미남이다.
Literally, this means "flowerly handsome." Many Korean women fantasize about their men being pretty and having girly faces. It's common to see popular Korean male singers dressed up and wearing makeup like women.

He / She is a...
Geuneun / Geunyeoneun ...ida.
그는 / 그녀는 ... 이다.

natural beauty.
jayeon mi-in
자연 미인

plastic surgery beauty.
seonghyeong mi-in
성형 미인

multitalented beauty.
palbangmi-in
팔방미인

This term refers to someone who is talented in many areas and also beautiful. You know, those people you want to hate but can't because they're also nice and gentle. Well, Koreans have a nice word for those nice people. (Personally, we hate them.)

pole, aka a tall person.
jeonbotdae
전봇대

string bean.
kkeokdari
꺽다리
This is someone so tall that they can be bent and still look tall.

fat ass.
ttungttaengi
뚱땡이

wild, sexy man.
yaseongnam
야성남
Though the metrosexual look is popular, the manly-man look has been gaining steam—thanks to a recent spate of seminude celebrities showing off their buff guns on TV.

He / She has...
Geuneun / Geunyeoneun…gajigoitda.
그는 / 그녀는 ... 가지고 있다.

a small face.
jageun eolgul
작은 얼굴을

a beautiful face.
eoljjang
얼짱
Literally, "face number one" or "face the best." *Eol* (얼) is shorthand for *eolgul* (얼굴; face), while *jjang* (짱) means "number one" or "the best."

You say, "She is the best face."
Guenye nuen eoljjang i da
(그녀는 얼짱이다).

a beautiful nose bridge.
ottokhan koreul
오똑한 코를

Have you seen any genetics-defying high and pointy noses on Korean friends in the U.S.? Korean noses are usually small and flat, so if you see a straight nose bridge leading up to a pointy nose tip (longer than two centimeters), it tells you one of two things. Either he or she is really lucky, or it's the beautiful product of a surgeon's scalpel.

big eyes.
keun nuneul
큰 눈을

long legs.
long darireul
롱 다리를

a great body. (voluptuous)
esseu line-eul
에스 라인을

an awesome body.
momjjang
몸짱

This is best said as "he is an awesome body"—*geuneun momjjangida* (그는 몸짱이다). Otherwise it just sounds cheesy.

a killer body.
aju jugineun momeul
아주 죽이는 몸을

big guns.
tantanhan pareul
딴딴한 팔을

washboard abs.
chocolate baereul
초콜렛 배를

This is when a guy has a six-pack that resembles a Hershey's chocolate bar.

honey thighs.
kkulbeokjireul
꿀벅지를

a six-pack.
sixpaekeul
씩스팩을

PLASTIC SURGERY

SUNGHYEONG SUSUL

성형 수술

Plastic surgery is really popular in Korea. It was considered shameful when people first started having it done back in the '80s, but today it's a lot more acceptable, and people are pretty open about their surgeries. This cosmetic boom was driven by widespread superficiality in a country with top-quality surgeons offering affordable prices. It's pretty common for parents to give their children plastic surgery as a graduation gift. But this is starting to have some creepy results now that many celebrities are becoming indistinguishable from one another.

Eyelid surgery
Ssangkapul susul
쌍가풀 수술
This surgery is the most common procedure Koreans use to look more "Western."

Nose job
Ko susul
코 수술

Boob job
Gaseum susul
가슴 수술

Lipo
Jibang heubipsul
지방흡입술

Botox
Botocs / jureum jegeo
보톡스 / 주름 제거

Did you go **under the knife**?
Neo eolgure ***kal dennya?***
너 얼굴에 **칼댔냐**?
There's a really gnarly video on YouTube of a Korean woman who became obsessed with plastic surgery and injected sesame oils into her face. It's gross. Check it out.

•••••The Korean ugly

Hangook poktan

한국 폭탄

In general, Koreans are a pretty sexy group of people. And if you had to choose just one nationality to sleep with for the rest of your life, you could do a lot worse. But despite the overall attractiveness of its people, Korea does harbor a few outliers. And by "outliers," I mean butt-ugly fatties that should never, ever reproduce.

He / She is...
Geuneun... / Geunyeoneun...
그는... / 그녀는...

unattractive.
mot saengyeotda.
못생겼다.

fugly.
maejuda.
메주다.
Literally, "fermented beans."

ugly-ass.
poktanida.
폭탄이다.
Literally, "bomb."

butt ugly.
hobakida.
호박이다.
Literally, "pumpkin."

too skinny.
bbijjeok mallatda.
삐쩍 말랐다.

anorexic.
angsanghage mallatda.
앙상하게 말랐다.

bony.
bbyeo bakke eopda.
뼈 밖에 없다.

unpopular.
ingiga eopda.
인기가 없다.

You are...
Neoneun...
너는...

an ugly man.
chunamida.
추남이다.

an ugly woman.
chunyeoda.
추녀다.

a fat boy. / a fat girl.
ttungboda. / ttungnyeoda.
뚱보다. / 뚱녀다.

a pig.
dwaejida.
돼지다.

a dwarf.
nanjaengida. / lujeoda.
난쟁이다. / 루저다.
On a popular TV show in Korea called *Minyeodeului Suda*, a female university student labeled any guys under 5' 6" as losers. Korean men were outraged! But the term stuck, and now all short men are called losers in Korea.

a fatso.
ttungttaengida.
뚱땡이다.

chubbier.
salijjeotda.
살이쪘다.

He / She has...
Geuneun / Geunyeoneun ... gajigo itda.
그는/그녀는...가지고 있다.

a big head. (applies to men)
keun daegarireul
큰 대가리를

a big face.
keun eolrgureul
큰 얼굴을

small eyes.
jageun nuneul
작은 눈을

big gut.
ttongbaereul
똥배를

a muffintop.
tubeu-reul ggyeosseo
튜브를 꼈어
Literally, "wearing an inner tube around your waist."

short legs.
shot dari / jangnong dari
숏 다리 / 장롱 다리

fat legs.
mudarireul
무다리를
Literally, "radish legs."

uneven ass cheeks.
jjak gungdaengireul
짝 궁댕이를

a fat ass.
ori gungdaengireul
오리 궁댕이를
Literally, "duck ass."

a saggy ass.
cheojin eongdeongireul
처진 엉덩이를

MORE UGLY KOREAN

These are popular Korean sayings used to make fun of others' appearances:

You are **small like a booger**!
Ko ttakji manhange kkabulgo isseo!
코 딱지 만한게 까불고 있어!

You are **small like a RAT**!
Jwisaekki manhange kkabulgo isseo!
쥐새끼 만한게 까불고 있어!

You **are the size of a dwarf's shit bag.**
Nanjaengi ttongjaru manhange kkabulgo isseo!
난쟁이 똥자루 만한게 까불고 있어!

Who wants to look at the uglyass!
Nuga jeogeo bondago?
누가 저거 본다고?

Pearl necklace on a pig's neck!
Dwaejimoge jinju mokgeori!
돼지목에 진주 목걸이.

You can't put lipstick on a **pig.**
Hobage jul geutneundago subak dwaenya?
호박에 줄 긋는다고 수박돼냐?
Literally, "Can pumpkins become watermelons with lines?" Koreans consider pumpkins ugly but watermelons handsome. So even if an ugly person puts on beautiful clothes, lots of makeup, and expensive, brand-name accessories, he or she will never be considered beautiful. At least, that's what they used to say—but if you spend your life savings on multiple plastic surgeries, you might just be able to get prettier.

Your legs are as short as a dresser's!
Neo wanjeon ***jangnong dariya!***
너 다리 완전 **장롱 다리야!**
Bend over and look at the bottom of your dresser. You'll see how small the space is between the ground and the dresser, since most dressers have short legs.

Holy shit, your head is the size of a watermelon!
Uwa, jenjang neo ***meoriga wanjeon subagiya!***
우와, 젠장, 너 **머리가 완전 수박이야!**
Korean watermelons are smaller than the ginormous fruits you see in US supermarkets—they're about the size of jack-o'-lantern pumpkins.

You have radish legs!
Neo wanjeon ***mudariya!***
너 완전 **무다리야!**
This is a popular saying used to insult girls who have short, fat legs.

•••••Piss
Ojum
오줌

Korea doesn't have many public restrooms. Lots of restaurants and bars share bathrooms and require a key to get in. Because of the scarcity of public johns, it's tough to find a nice place to pop a squat. So you'd better learn the following phrases to show how bad you gotta use it!

Where's the can?
Hwajangsi*ri eodiyeyo?*
화장실이 어디예요?

I need to piss bad!
Ojum *maryuh!*
오줌 마려!

I ...
Na ...
나...

gotta pee.
ojum *ssayahae.*
오줌 싸야해.

gotta **piss.**
swi *ssayahae.*
쉬 싸야해.

gotta **take a leak.**
mul ***bbaeyahae.***
물 **빼야해.**

Can you pass me some **TP**?
Hyuji *jom gatda jullae?*
휴지 좀 갖다 줄래?
There are sometimes vending machines outside of public restrooms to provide toiletries.

Shit, I missed the mark and **pissed all over** my hands.
A sipal, jojun jal motaeseo ***sone ojum da mudeosseo.***
아 시팔, 조준 잘 못해서 **손에 오줌 다 묻었어.**
It's common to witness public urination on the sidewalk at night when men are shit-faced drunk.

My **bladder** is about to explode!
Ojumbbo *teojilgeo gata!*
오줌보 터질거 같아!

Are you going **number 1** or **number 2**?
Neo ***keungeo jageungeo****?*
너 **큰거 작은거**?
Literally, "Are you going big or small?"

•••••Shit

Ttong

똥

Feces
Daebyeon
대변

SHITTY SAYINGS

TTONGMAL

똥말

It seems that every culture has its own sayings about shit that can confuse the hell out of foreigners. For instance, what would an F.O.B. Korean think if you told him that he was "full of shit" or that his haircut was "the shit"? It's no different in Korea, where they have their own special phrases. So keep your ears peeled for these colloquial nuggets.

The pot calling the kettle black.
Literal translation: "The dog smeared in shit criticizes the dog smeared in foliage."
Ttong mudeun gaega gyeo mudeun gaebogo mora handa.
똥묻은 개가 겨묻은 개보고 뭐라한다.

Na ttong bbujijik bbujijik ssasseo.
나 똥 뿌지직 뿌지직 쌌어.
There's no good English translation for this, since it's simply the onomatopoeic sound of shit coming out of your butthole. Saying it basically means that you just took a shit.

You are the shit! (Used sarcastically.)
Neo jalnasseo, ne ttong gulgeo!
너 잘났어, 네 똥 굵어!
This is a mocking and sarcastic backhanded compliment.

I can't eat any more; my stomach is full of **shit.**
Deoisang mot meogeo, ***ttong****euro chasseo.*
더이상 못 먹어, **똥**으로 찼어.
This one pretty much speaks for itself.

Poop
Eunga
응가

Do you want to go poo poo?
Eunga *halkka?*
응가 할까?
Mothers often say to their babies, "Let's poo poo together!"

I am about to **shit in my pants.**
Bajie ttong ssalgeot *gata.*
바지에 똥 쌀것 같아.

I have to take a…
Na … ssayahae.
나 … 싸야해.

dump.
han mudeogi
한무더기

shit.
ttong
똥

I have **diarrhea.**
*Na **seolssa**hae.*
나 설사해.

•••••Fart / Burp

Bangu / Teureum
방구 / 트름

By American standards, it's considered rude to fart or burp in public, but for Koreans it's just a natural bodily occurrence. (Well, at least burping is; farting is still kinda frowned upon.) So don't look surprised when the elderly Korean gentleman in the booth next to you belches kimchi in your face.

Who **farted?**
Bangu *nuga ggyeosseo?*
방구 누가 꼈어?

That **stinks.**
Naemsae juginda.
냄새 죽인다.

Your **ass** is playing the flute!
***Eongdeong**-iga pirireul bune!*
엉덩이가 피리를 부네!

Smells like a **rotten egg.**
***Sseogeun dalgyal** naemsaena.*
썩은 달걀 냄새나.

Your **fart** smells like old rotten kimchi.
*Ni **bangu** orae mugeun kimchi naemsaena.*
니 **방구** 오래 묵은 김치 냄새 나.

Burp
Teureum
트름

It's not considered rude for elders to burp at restaurants in Korea. However, if you're a youngster, you'd better keep such skills under wraps until you're with your friends.

> Don't **burp** in front of me, you nasty shit.
> ***Tereum** hajima, deoreowun saekki.*
> **트름**하지마 더러운 새끼.

Hiccups
Ttalkkukjil
딸꾹질

Boogers
Kottakji
코딱지

In Korean, "boogers" is a combination of the words "nose" and "scalp."

> Quit picking your **boogers.**
> ***Kottakji** jom geuman pa.*
> **코딱지** 좀 그만 파.

Snot
Konmul
콧물

Wipe the **snot** off your face.
***Konmul** jom dagga.*
콧물 좀 닦아.

Blow your nose.
***Ko** jom pureo.*
코 좀 풀어.

Eye boogers
Nunkkop
눈꼽

You have **eye boogers**!
*Neo **nunkkop** kkyeosseo!*
너 **눈꼽**꼈어!

Earwax
Gwiji / Gwitbab
귀지 / 귓밥

Gwijigae are good for taking out your earwax.
***Gwijigae**ro gwiji paneunge joa.*
귀지개로 귀지 파는게 좋아.

Gwijigae is a tool made of either wood or metal. It resembles a long, thin spoon and is used to clean out earwax.

·····Sickness
Byeong
병

I'm not feeling well.
Momi anjoa.
몸이 안좋아.

I am **sick.**
Na ***apeo.***
나 **아퍼**.

I'm **hurt.**
Na ***dacheosseo.***
나 **다쳤어**.

I am going **to die.**
Na ***jugeul geo gata.***
나 **죽을 거 같아**.
Not literally—this is a hyperbole expressing intense illness.

I think I caught a **cold.**
Gamgi *geollin geo gata.*
감기 걸린 거 같아.

Are you **okay?**
Neo ***gwenchana?***
너 **괜찮아**?

Where does it **hurt?**
Eodi ***apeo?***
어디 **아퍼**?

You don't look **too hot.**
Byeollo ***an joa*** *boyeo.*
별로 **안 좋아** 보여.

You are **pale.**
Eolguri ***changbaekhae.***
얼굴이 **창백해**.

I have a **stomachache.**
Na ***baeapeo.***
나 **배아퍼**.

I'm having **my period.**
Na ***saengrijungiya.***
나 **생리중이야**.

I'm on the **rag.**
***Geunari**ya.*
그날이야.

I have raging **PMS.**
*Na saengri jeonira **piemesseu**ro jirariya.*
나 생리전이라 **피엠에스**로 지랄이야.

I have a **fever.**
***Yeolna**.*
열나.

Call 119.
Iliilgue jeonhwahae.
일일구에 전화해.
In Korea, 119 is what you call to get the fire department.

·····Pharmacy

Yakguk

약국

Koreans practice a lot of Eastern medicine, but it's pretty easy to find more Westernized treatment and get the meds that you're used to.

Where are you hurting?
Eodiga apeoyo?
어디가 아퍼요?

Can you give me some **headache medicine**?
***Geborin** juseyo?*
게보린 주세요?
This is basically Tylenol (acetaminophen).

Aspirin
Aspirin
아스피린

Ibuprofen
Ebupropen
이부프로펜

Cold medicine
Gamgiyak
감기약 (*brand*—판프린 에프)

Bug bite medicine
Mogiyak
모기약 (파스—*for mosquito bites*)
This is hydrocortisone.

TUMS
Baetalyak
배탈약 (*brand*—훼스탈)

Antidiarrheal medication
Seolsayak
설사약 (*brand*—정로환)

Korean brand of energy drink, like Red Bull
Bakaseu
박카스

Band-Aid
Banchango
반창고

Neosporin
Madekasol, husidin
마데카솔, 후시딘

Chinese herbal medicine ball
Wuhwangcheongsimwon
우황 청심원
This curative is made from a bunch of Chinese herbs rolled into a small ball. It stinks like hell but can cure you instantly when you are in mental or physical shock.

> **I'm in shock! I need a Chinese medicine ball!**
> *Na nollasseo! Wuhwang cheongsimwon pilyohae!*
> 나 놀랐어! 우황청심원 필요해!

CHAPTER 6

HORNY KOREAN

HANGUKESEO SSEUNEUN YAHANMAL

한국에서 쓰는 야한말

•••••Sex

Sex / Sungwangye

섹스 / 성관계

Like most people, Koreans have getting laid on their minds 24/7. Talking openly about sex, however, is a different story. It's still pretty taboo. And when it does happen, it's usually as an embarrassed euphemism or in English, because talking dirty just comes more naturally in English.

Thanks to the internet (i.e., porn), lots of new sexual terms are starting to flood the language. So your Korean friends will probably understand you when you start to explain your *bukkake* fetish. But what are Koreans to do with this newfound sexual awakening? Most Koreans live with their parents until they tie the knot, so bringing home a booty call to try out their new reverse-blumpkin moves is out of the question.

That's where the "love motel" (러브 모텔) comes in. Such rendezvous points may sound sleazy to Westerners but are a fact of life for unmarried Asians. Here you can fuck without having to worry about Mom or Dad walking in and seeing you punching mochi all night long. Surprisingly, the motels are often chic and well decorated, and they only cost about $40 to $50 a day. But for some reason, most people use them for just a couple of hours, re-creating all the poses they see in the FREE in-room porn.

I want to sleep with you.
*Na neorang **jagosipeo**.*
나 너랑 **자고싶어**.

I want to do it with you.
*Na neorang **hagosipeo**.*
나 너랑 **하고싶어**.

I'm getting in the mood to...
Na ... hagosipeo.
나 ... 하고싶어.

make love.
sarangeul nanugo
사랑을 나누고

•••••Cocks

Geosigi

거시기

Whoever said "It's not the size of the boat but the motion of the ocean" was full of shit. Bigger is better. Less is not more. And because a big Johnson is so important, there are lots of ways to describe one.

Penis
Mulgeon
물건

My penis is thicker than yours.
Nae mulgeon-i nikkeoboda deo gulgeo.
내 물건이 니꺼보다 더 굵어.

Baby penis
Gochu
고추

This term is used when adults comment on a baby boy's penis, a frequent occurrence in Korea since it's very popular to take young boys to public bathhouses.

Your baby penis is very handsome.
I nomeui jasik ***gochu*** *cham jal saengyeotnae.*
이 놈의 자식, **고추** 참 잘 생겼네.

Foreskin
Kkeopjil
껍질

Did you remove your foreskin?
Neo jaji ***kkeopjjil*** *kkannya?*
너 자지 **껍질** 깠냐?

Circumcise
Pogyeong susul
포경수술

To hunt whales (*goraejabi*; 고래잡이) is a euphemism that comes from coincidental homonyms—*pogyeong susul* (to circumcise) and *pogyeong-up* (whaling).

Can I lick your... ?
... haltado doe?
...핥아도 돼?

Can I spank your...?
... chyeodo doe?
... 쳐도 돼?

Can I suck your...?
... bbarado doe?
...빨아도 돼?

Can I take a picture of your...?
... geogi sajin jjigeodo doe?
...거기 사진 찍어도 돼?

Don't touch my...
... manjijima.
...만지지마.

I love...
... na joahae
...나 좋아해

Wow, that is one fantastic...
Uwa, ... geugeo jeongmal juginda.
우와, ... 그거 정말 죽인다.

I've never seen a ... like that.
Hanbeondo ... bonjeogi eopsseo.
한번도 ... 본적이 없어.

cock
jaji
자지

Johnson
namgeun
남근

dick
eumkyeong
음경

wiener
jot
좆

erection
balttak seon jaji
발딱 선 자지

boner
ttakttakhan jaji
딱딱한 자지

head
guidu
귀두

nuts
gohwan
고환

nads
eumnang
음낭

balls
bural
불알

rim of the head
jaji kkeut
자지 끝

pubes (male)
jaji teol
자지 털

•••••Tits and ass

Gaseumirang eongdeongi

가슴이랑 엉덩이

Tits, boobies, knockers, melons, breasts, tatas, and fun bags—no matter what you call them, they're awesome. More awesome than a sweet ass, though? That's a debate that philosophers have long argued but never settled. Yet can't we all agree that both are magical in their own special way? From my girlfriends' experiences (and mine…can't deny it), we've come up with the following tendencies: American boys go for the asses when they kiss girls, and Korean boys—as awkward as the position can be—go for the boobies. Damn mama's boys!

I love big…
Nan keun …ga joa.
난 큰 …가 좋아.

Can I squeeze your…?
Ne … jumul-leodo dwae?
네 … 주물러도 돼?

Fondle my…
Nae … manjeojo.
내 … 만져줘.

Pinch my…
…kkojibeojo.
…꼬집어줘.

Show me your…
… boyeohjobwa.
…보여줘봐.

tits.
gaseum
가슴

nipples.
jeotkkokji
젖꼭지

ass.
eongdeongi
엉덩이

asshole.
ttonkkumeong
똥구멍

anus.
hangmun
항문

THE BOOBY CONTINUUM

GAJI GAJI GASEUMDEUL
가지 가지 가슴들

Breastless
Aseupalteue buteun kkumttakji
아스팔트에 붙은 껌딱지
Literally, "flat gum on an asphalt street." You will see this on many Korean girls, who are stick-thin anyway.

Flat-chested
Jeollbyeok
절벽

Barely-breasted
Binyakhan gaseum
빈약한 가슴

Medium-breasted
Adamhan gaseum
아담한 가슴

Ample-breasted
Geullaemeo
글래머

Big tits
Geoyu
거유

Ginormous tits
Jeotso
젓소
Literally, "milking cow."

Beautiful tits
Chakhan gaseum
착한 가슴
Literally, "nice breasts." In Korea, a beautiful appearance makes you a "nice person." Therefore, if you have beautiful tits, guys will call you nice and kind. Works out, doesn't it?

Fake boobs
Bbongaseum
뽕가슴

•••••Pussy time!

Boji sigan!
보지 시간!

Though they may be "all pink on the inside," there remain a plethora of terms to describe the female vajajay.

I want to lick your...
Na neo ... halko sipeo.
나 너 ... 핥고싶어.

Eat my...
Nae ... meogeojwo.
내 ... 먹어줘.

Fingerbang my...
Nae ... soneuro bagajo.
내 ... 손으로 박아줘.

I'm going to ravage your...
Naega ni ... mangateurilkkeoya.
내가 니 ... 망가뜨릴꺼야.

pussy.
boji
보지

cunt.
jil
질

hairy pussy.
teol maneun boji
털많은 보지
Don't expect to see Brazilians when you hook up with chicks in Korea. A hairy pussy is the norm here.

shaved pussy.
baekboji
백보지
Literally, "blank pussy."

clitoris.
eumhaek
음핵

clit.
clitoris
크리토리스

love button.
kong
콩
Literally, "bean." Losing your virginity is *kongkkagi* (콩까기)—"peeling the bean."

g-spot.
ji spot
지스팟

> **Where is your g-spot?**
> *Neoji spotsi eohdiya?*
> 너 지스팟이 어디야?

pubes. (female)
bojiteol
보지털

pussy juice
aeaek
애액

••••••Sexual acts
Seongyo
성교

Sometimes missionary sex just won't cut it. Sometimes you just feel the need to go all reverse cowgirl and fingerbang your lover's butthole during a mid-afternoon gangbang. It's perfectly natural. There's no need to be ashamed of your female ejaculation while your boyfriend tittyfucks you in the midst of a Cleveland steamer. Everybody does it.

I am at a **perverted** age now.
*Nado **jingeureowun** naiya.*
나도 **징그러운** 나이야.

Have you ever had anal sex?
Thongkkoro haebwasseo?
똥꼬로 해 봤어?

I want to do some...
...hago sipeo.
...하고 싶어.

I'm tired of...
... haneungeon jaemiupsseo.
... 하는건 재미없어.

kissing.
Bbobbo
뽀뽀

Give me a **kiss** to remember!
*Oneureul ginyeom halmanhan **bbobbo**haejwo!*
오늘을 기념 할만한 **뽀뽀**해줘!

French kiss.
Kiss
키스

foreplay.
Aemu
애무

skinship.
Skinship
스킨쉽

fingerbanging.
Soneuro
손으로

Finger me!
Soneuro haejwo!
손으로 해줘!

cunnilingus.
Yeoseong gugang aemu
여성 구강 애무

Go down on me.
Ibeuro haejwo.
입으로 해줘.

fellatio.
Namseong gugang aemu
남성 구강 애무

Give me a blow job.
Ibeuro haejwo.
입으로 해줘.

Wanna try...?
...haeboja?
... 해보자?

I like...
Nan ... joahae.
난 ... 좋아해.

swallowing.
samkidanuengirl
삼키는걸

cumming on the face.
eolgurae ssaneungirl
얼굴에 싸는걸

sixty-nine.
yukgu
육구

titty-fucking.
gaseum sex
가슴 섹스

missionary style.
apchigi
앞치기

doggy-style.
dwichigi
뒤치기

woman on top.
maltagi
말타기
Literally, "riding horse."

Threesome
Sseurisseom
쓰리썸

Group sex
Group sex
그룹 섹스

Gangbang
Dollimbbang
돌림빵

Anal
Aeneol
애널

Do it in my asshole.
Ttonkkumeongeuro haejwo.
똥구멍으로 해줘.

Female ejaculation
Yeoseong sajeong
여성 사정

•••••Orgasm
Oreugajeum
오르가즘

Do it...
...hae.
...해.

faster, faster.
Bballi bballi
빨리 빨리

slower.
Cheoncheonhi
천천히

harder.
Ssege
세게

softer.
Salsal
살살

more.
Deo
더

This hurts.
Apa.
아파.

This feels really good.
Gibun joa.
기분 좋아.

I'm getting a hard-on.
Seosseo.
섰어.

I'm starting to get off.
Neukkimi wa.
느낌이 와.

I want to come.
Ssago sipeo.
싸고 싶어.

I'm about to come.
Ssallyeogo geurae.
쌀려고 그래.

Where do you want it?
Eodiro hallae?
어디로 할래?

I'm coming!
Na ssalkeogata!
나 쌀거같아!

Did you have an orgasm?
Neo neukkyeosseo?
너 느꼈어?
Literally, "Did you feel it?"

I just came all over.
Bangeum ssasseo.
방금 쌌어.

I had a wet dream.
Na mongjeong haesseo.
나 몽정했어.

I need to beat off. (male)
Na ttalttari chyeoyahae.
나 딸딸이 쳐야해.

Go masturbate.
Jawihae.
자위해.

·····Sexcessories
Sex toy
섹스토이

Do you have a ...?
~isseo?
~있어?

Let's try using a...
~sseoboja.
~써보자.

condom.
Condom
콘돔

Do you have a condom?
*Neo **condom** gajigo isseo?*
너 **콘돔** 가지고 있어?

dildo.
Dildo
딜도

Where can I get a dildo?
*Neo **dildo** eodieseo guhae?*
너 **딜도** 어디에서 구해?

vibrator.
Baibeureiteo
바이브레이터

Do you like my fingers or your vibrator better?
Neo nae songaragi joa anim ***baibeureiteo****ro haneunge deo joa?*
너 내 손가락이 좋아 아님 **바이브레이터**로 하는게 더 좋아?

Let's watch...
... boja.
... 보자.

porn.
Poreuno
포르노
It's illegal to film porn in Korea, but you can import it from abroad. A while ago, some high school students filmed themselves having sex and made a video called *Red Scarf* (*bbalgan mahoora*; 빨간 마후라). The video got leaked and became a big deal in Korea.

adult video.
Adult video
어덜트 비디오
These films are usually found in Korean love motels. Unfortunately, they're pretty tame compared to American porn (you don't even get to see any pussy or cock—lame!).

•••••Your sexuality
Neoeui seonghyang
너의 성향

Scholars often talk about the virgin-whore dichotomy of women's sexuality. But what about the butch-fem polarity and the pimp-ho binary? Where do all the call-girls, players, born-again virgins, bisexuals, premature ejaculators, and S&M freaks fit into the spectrum? Well, in the wide world of Korean slang, there's a place for all you freaky sex fiends. So come on in. It's warm in here.

I love a good slut.
*Naneun **geolle** joahae.*
나는 **걸레** 좋아해.

I'm a...
Naneun ...ya.
나는 ... 야.

virgin.
cheonyeo
처녀

ancient virgin.
cheonyeonkinyeommul
천연기념물
Known as a "national treasure" or "never been kissed," for both boys and girls.

30-something unmarried woman.
nocheonyeo
노처녀

whore.
changnyeo
창녀

call girl.
call geol
콜걸

underage prostitute.
wonjogyoje
원조교제

Homosexual
Dongseongaeja
동성애자

Gay
Geyi
게이

Lesbian
Lejeubieon
레즈비언

Bisexual
Yangseongaeja
양성애자

Queer
Horosaekki
호로새끼

Pimp
Gidungseobang
기둥서방

Playboy
Baramdungi
바람둥이

Quickdraw
Tokki
토끼
Literally, "rabbit."

Premature ejaculation
Joru
조루

Impotent
Balgibujeon
발기부전

Sadist
Saedist
세디스트

Masochist
Maesokist
메소키스트

Pervert
Byeontae
변태

Two-timer
Yangdari
양다리

Player
Muneodari
문어다리

> **Did you hear? That player got an STD from sleeping around.**
> *Waeniriya, jeonom* ***muneodari*** *geolchidaga seongbyeong ormatde.*
> 왠일이야, 저놈 **문어다리** 걸치다가 성병 옮았데.

CHAPTER 7

ANGRY KOREAN

HANGUK YOK

한국 욕

Just because Koreans are smaller than your average white dude doesn't mean they get pushed around. They can be some badass motherfuckers. And what they lack in size they make up for with an impressive array of insults, swear words, smackdowns, and verbal abuse directed toward the size of their enemy's genitals. You've been warned.

••••••Enemies

Jeok

적

I hate my...

Nan nae ...ga sireo

난 내 ... 가 싫어

boss.

sangsa

상사

I'm so mad at my asshole boss.

*Geu **sangsa** gaesaekkittaemune yeolbada jukkesseo.*

그 **상사** 개새끼때문에 열받아 죽겠어.

rival.
waensu
왠수

I'm fucked because of my rival.
*Na geu **waensu**ttaemune jot dwaesseo.*
나 그 **왠수**때문에 좆 됐어.

My…is a real asshole.
Nae …neun jinjja sibalnomiya.
내 … 는 진짜 시발놈이야.

ex-girlfriend
jeon yeochin
전 여친

My ex-girlfriend is a slut.
*Nae **jeon yeoichin** ssibalnyeon.*
내 **전 여친** 씨 발 년.

ex-boyfriend
jeon namchin
전 남친

My ex-boyfriend is a psycho.
*Nae **jeon namchin** michinnom. / ttorai.*
내 전 남친 미친놈. / 또라이.

teacher (unpopular) / any older person trying to preach
kkondae
꼰대

My shitty teacher tried to say that I didn't do my homework.
*Nae **kkondae**ga nabogo sookjereul an haetdaneun geoya.*
내 **꼰대**가 나보고 숙제를 안 했다는 거야.

mother-in-law
sieomeoni (husband's mom) / jangmonim (wife's mom)
시어머니 / 장모님

My mother-in-law has lost her mind.
***Si-eomeoni** nomang nasyeosseo.*
시어머니 노망 나셨어.

Politician
Jeongchi-in
정치인

All politicians are con artists.
***Jungchi-indeur**eun da sagikkuniya.*
정치인들은 다 사기꾼이야.

Police
Gyeongchal
경찰

Cops
Jjapsae
짭새

Shit, the cops are coming.
*Ssibal, **jjapsae** tteotda.*
씨발 **짭새** 떳다.

••••• Pissed off
Yeolbatda
열받다

Sometimes shit pisses you off. It's important to know the proper verbiage in order to fully convey this emotion to those around you. Otherwise you may have to cut a bitch.

Damn!
Bireomeogeul!
빌어먹을!

Shit!
Jenjang!
젠장!

Fuck!
Ssibal!
씨발!

I'm in a bad mood today, so don't get on my nerves!
*Oneul na **gibun ggulggul**hanikka geondeulji ma!*
오늘 나 **기분 꿀꿀**하니까 건들지 마!

Get away from me!
Kkeojeo!
꺼져!

Don't make me angry!
***Yeol batge** hajima!*
열 받게 하지마!

I'm going to kill you!
***Jugyeo**beorinda!*
죽여버린다!
This is a popular phrase used lightly, and normally it's not life threatening.

Leave me alone.
Geunyang naebido.
그냥 내비둬.

I'm so pissed off!
King-bahd-jee!
킹받지
Literally, receiving the "King of anger."

Whatever!
Uhjjuhlteebee!
어쩔티비
Korea's Generation Z likes to abbreviate. This is shortened from "어쩌라고 티비나 봐~"—which means "Mind your business and just watch TV!"

I didn't ask, nor am I curious.
Anmul angoong.
안물안궁

None of your business!
Gwansimggeo!
관심꺼!

Don't worry about me!
Sangwanma!
상관마!

You're bothering me!
Gwichana!
귀찮아!

You're so annoying!
Jjajeungna!
짜증나!

You're *pissing me off* with your whining!
*Neoga jjingjjingdaeseo **jjangna**!*
너가 찡찡대서 **짱나**!

My head is about to *explode*!
***Ttukkeong yeollinda**!*
뚜껑 열린다!
Literally, "My pot cover is about to boil open."

•••••Smack talk

Yokseol
욕설

Koreans like to talk shit, and the most commonly used insult is "crazy." Whenever you come across someone who pisses you off, calling them crazy under your breath is a great way to warm up your shit-talking. Whoever comes up with the most creative smack talk about the other person's appearance/hygiene/mother's dirty sex life is the winner!

That bitch is crazy!
Jeo nyeon ***michin nyeon****iya!*
저년 **미친년**이야!

You're a punk ass.
Meorie pido an mareunge.
머리에 피도 안 마른게.
Literally, "Your head is still blood-wet from your mom's womb."

RACISTS

INJONGCHABYEOLJA

인종차별자

People often assume that South Koreans don't like North Koreans, but the truth is that North Koreans are often the friends and family of their neighbors to the south. The people Koreans really hate are the Japanese. Japan colonized Korea for 35 years until 1945. That tends to breed hostility. Other than the Japanese, Koreans are ready to insult everybody with pretty much equal opportunity.

Get outta my face, you dumb ...
Jeolluu ggeojeo, i meojeori gateun ...
적루 꺼져, 이 머저리같은...

Yankee.
yangki.
양키.

Japs. (Japanese)
Jjokbari. / Ilbonnom. / Woenom.
쪽발이. / 일본놈. / 왜놈.

How is it possible to be so stupid?
Eotteoke geureoke ***babo****ilsuga innya?*
어떻게 그렇게 **바보**일수가 있냐?

What a moron!
Meogcheogi *saekki!*
멍청이 새끼!

She's such a bitch!
Jeoreon gae gateun nyeon!
저런 개같은 년!

Son of a bitch!
Gaesaekki!
개새끼!

I'm gonna beat up that **asshole.**
*Jeo **ssibalnom** pae jugilggeoya.*
저 **씨발놈** 패 죽일꺼야.

Rude people suck.
***Ssagagi upneun** nom / nyeon jaesu eopsseo.*
싸가지 없는 놈 / 년 재수없어.

Does lusting after Miley Cyrus make me a **bad person**?
*Miley Cyrus joahamyeon na **nabbeunnom**inya?*
마일리 싸이러스 좋아하면 나 **나쁜놈**이냐?

He's nothing but **trash.**
*Jeo saekkineun **sseuregi** bakke andwae.*
저 새끼는 **쓰레기** 밖에 안돼.

I hate **rotten people!**
***Sseogeul nomdeul** neomu sireo!*
썩을 놈들 너무 싫어!

She has a **bad attitude.**
*Jeonyeon **seongkkal deureoweo**.*
저년 **성깔 드러워**.

You're **nuts!**
***Ttorai**gateun!*
또라이 같은!

Quit being such a **bastard!**
***Horosaekki** gateun jit jom geumanhae!*
호로새끼 같은 짓 좀 그만해!

Don't be a crybaby!
***Ulbo**jit hajima!*
울보짓 하지마!

> **Santa won't give a gift to a crybaby.**
> *Santaneun Ulbohante sunmul an jundae.*
> 산타는 울보한테 선물 안 준대.
> Korean mothers use this saying when trying to convince their whiny kids to shut up.

Cheapskate
Jjandori / Jjansuni
짠돌이 / 짠순이

> **Your boyfriend is a cheapskate.**
> *Neo namjachinguneun neomu **jjandori**ya.*
> 너 남자친구는 너무 **짠돌이**야.

> **Pay it, you cheapskate!**
> *Don jom sseo, **jjandora**!*
> 돈 좀써, **짠돌아**!

You're so foul-mouthed.
Neon ibe geolle mureosseo.
넌 입에 걸레 물었어.
Literally, "You have a dirty rag in your mouth!"

Your dad is a pervert.
*Neone abba **byeontae**ya.*
너네 아빠 **변태**야.

That bullshitter always makes shit up.
*Jeo **heopungjaengi** mennal geojitmalhae.*
저 **허풍쟁이** 맨날 거짓말해.

Japanese girls are low class.
*Ilbonnyeondeureun **ssangnyeon**deuriya.*
일본년들은 **쌍년**들이야.

That stalker won't stop texting me.
*Jeo **stokeo**ga gyesok munjahae.*
저 **스토커**가 계속 문자해.

You're fucking bad luck.
*Neo jinjja **jaesu upsseop**.*
너 진짜 **재수없어**.

Korean dudes are lazy.
*Hanguk namjadeul g**e-eureumbaengi**deuriya.*
한국 남자애들 **게으름뱅이**들이야.

Men are pigs.
*Namjaneun da **dwaeji**ya.*
남자는 다 **돼지**야.

You're worthless.
*Neon **sseulmo upneun** nomiya.*
넌 **쓸모 없는** 놈이야.

You're a parasite.
*Ya i **bindaesaekki**ya.*
야 이 **빈대새끼**야.

••••••Snapping
Nun doragannae
눈 돌아갔네

Believe it or not, more than half of Koreans are blood type B. That means that they're prone to being short-tempered, according to a wacky but well-known Korean blood-type personality test. So whenever you see someone's eyes go all crazy and they start barking at you for no reason, you can escalate the situation by inferring that they are blood type B and have no control over their emotions. Koreans just love hearing this.

Snapping
Nun dorogannae
눈 돌아갔네
Literally, "Your eyes have gone crazy."

Careful, dude's about to **snap.**
*Josimhae, je **nun doragaryeogohae.***
조심해, 제 **눈 돌아가려고해**.

He's got a real **short temper.**
*Je jinjja **dahyeoljil**iya.*
제 진짜 **다혈질**이야.

Uh-oh, she's starting to get **standoffish.**
*Jeobwa, jyae **bbeoljjumhaejinja**.*
저봐, 재 **뻘쭘해진다**.

He's giving you the **glare.**
*Jyaega neo **noryeobwa**.*
재가 너 **노려봐**.

Are you giving me a **dirty look**?
*Neo na **jjaeryeobonya**?*
너 나 **째려보냐**?

Are you **insane**?
*Neo **dorannya**?*
너 **돌았냐**?

You're **fucking hella crazy**! (dramatizing)
*Neo **jonna dorasseo**!*
너 **존나 돌았어**!

Lower your eyes!
***Nun kkara** i gaesaekkiya!*
눈깔아 이 개새끼야!
It's considered extremely disrespectful to look elders straight in their eyes while they are lecturing you.

I'm about to **explode.**
*Na **teojigi** ilbojikjeoniya.*
나 **터지기** 일보 직전이야.

My life is fucked.
*Nae **paljjaga gaepaljjaya**.*
내 팔자가 개상팔자야.

……Fighting words
Ssaulttae sseuneun maldeul
싸울때 쓰는 말들

Guns are illegal in Korea. They're for the military only. So how do Korean cops protect themselves and fight the bad guys? Why, with whistles and sticks, of course! This may sound wussy to you, but I wouldn't mess with a Korean cop! Those sticks can pack a mean hit. But if you do fight a cop, or anyone else for that matter, here are some good terms to really push the situation to full-scale violence.

I don't like you.
Neo sireo.
너 싫어.

I hate you.
Neo miwo.
너 미워

You suck!
Neo wang jesu!
너 왕 재수!

Go away!
Jeoriga!
저리가!

Go to hell.
Jiokga!
지옥가!

Fuck off!
Ggeojyeo!
꺼져!

Fuck you.
Yeotmugeo. / Bbeokyu.
엿먹어. / 뻑큐.

Shut your mouth.
Agari dakchyeo.
아가리 닥쳐.

Shut the fuck up.
Dakchyeo.
닥쳐.

Do you want to die?
Jugeullae!
죽을래!
This isn't a real-life threat; it's used more commonly as playful smack talk.

What the fuck?
Ssibal igeo moya?
시발 이거 뭐야?

What did you just say?
Dasi malhaebwa?
다시 말해봐?

Let's take it outside.
Bakkeuro nawa.
밖으로 나와.

Bring it on!
Wa! / Haebwa.
와! / 해봐.

You got a problem?
Bulman isseo?
불만 있어?

You picking a fight with me for no reason?
I saram hwangdanghage saramjapne?
이 사람 황당하게 사람잡네?

I'm gonna fuck you up.
*Neo **jugeuljul ara**.*
너 **죽을줄 알아**.

I'm gonna kick your ass.
*Neo **jonna majeuljul ara**.*
너 **존나 맞을줄알아**.

I'm gonna beat the shit out of you.
*Neo gae paedeusi **majeuljul ara**.*
너 개 패듯이 **맞을줄 알아**.
Literally, "I'm going to beat you up like a dog." This originates from the Korean practice of eating dog meat. To prepare the delicacy, the live canine is beaten with a bat to tenderize the meat. I know, I know, it's morbid, especially if you're PETA vegetarian. Eating dog meat is now banned in Korea.

Kneel or die, bitch!
Gaenyeon, an kkureumyeon jukneunda!
개년, 안 꿇으면 죽는다!

I fucked him up!
Jeo saekki yut mugyeosseo!
저 새끼 엿먹였어!

·····Stopping a fight
Ssaum jungjisikigi
싸움 중지시키기

So you're at a bar getting tipsy and talkin' shit about some dude's slutty sister. Next thing you know, dude's got ten friends and all of your crew has dipped out on you like a bunch of pussies. Time to make nice and kiss some proverbial ass.

Hey, let's...
Ya, uri...
야, 그만 ...

relax.
jinjeonghae.
진정해.

compromise.
hwahaehae.
화해해.

calm down.
hwanaeji ma.
화내지 마.

I'm sorry.
Mianhae.
미안해.

I apologize.
Sagwa halgge.
사과할께.

It's my fault.
Naega jalmot haesseo.
내가 잘못 했어.

You should understand me!
Neoga ihaehae!
너가 이해해!

Forgive me.
Yongseohaejo.
용서해줘.

Give me one more chance.
Hanbeonman bwajwo.
한번만 봐줘.

Forget about it.
Ijeo beoryeo.
잊어 버려.

It has nothing to do with me.
Narang sangwan eopneun iriya.
나랑 상관 없는 일이야.

Stop it.
Geumanhae.
그만해.

Don't do it.
Hajima.
하지마.

It's already in the past.
Da jinan iriya.
다 지난 일이야.

Whatever.
Dwaesseo.
됐어.

Don't go.
Gagima!
가지마!

I'm going to call the cops.
Jjapsae bureunda.
짭새 부른다.

Call 112!
Singohanda!
신고한다!
"112" is the emergency number for calling the cops in Korea.

CHAPTER 8

SPORTY KOREAN

HANGUK SPORTS YONGEO

한국 스포츠 용어

Koreans are some of the most competitive people in the world, so they don't mess around when it comes to sports. Soccer is big, and anybody who watches the Olympics will know that Koreans kick some serious ass in speed skating. They clean up golds in this sport like nobody's business.

••••••Sports

Sports / Undong

스포츠 / 운동

Do you like sports?
Neo ***undong*** *joahae?*
너 **운동** 좋아해?

What sport do you play?
Neo eotteon ***undong*** *jalhae?*
너 어떤 **운동** 잘해?

What's your team?
Neo nugu ***pyeon****iya?*
너 누구 **편**이야?

Whose team are you on?
*Neo nae **pyeon**iya je pyeoniya?*
너 내 **편**이야 제 편이야?

Who's your favorite player?
*Niga jel joahaneun **sunsu**ga nuguya?*
니가 젤 좋아하는 **선수**가 누구야?

Let's watch...
Uri ... boja.
우리 ... 보자.

Let's play...
Uri ... haja.
우리 ... 하자.

basketball.
nongu
농구

baseball.
yagu
야구

Strike
Heot swing
헛 스윙

Home run
Home run
홈런

volleyball.
baegu
배구

golf.
golf
골프

Let's go...
Uri ... hareo gaja.
우리 ... 하러 가자.

running.
dalligi
달리기

I have a cramp in my leg!
Darie jwinasseo!
다리에 쥐났어!

Do you want to go for a run?
*Uri **ttwilkka**?*
우리 **뛸**까?

I'm out of breath!
Na sumcha!
나 숨차!

swimming.
suyeong
수영

swimming pool
suyeongjang
수영장

Tae-hwan Park really tears it up in the pool!
Park Tae-hwan jinjja mulkkaeya!
박태환 진짜 물개야!
Literally, "Tae-hwan Park is a seal!" Tae-hwan Park is the Michael Phelps of Korea. He has several Olympic gold medals and world champion titles.

Billiards
Dangu
당구

Let's go for a game of billiards.
Dangu hanpan hareo gaja.
당구 한판 하러 가자.

Inline skating
Inline skate
인라인 스케이트

Bicycling
Jajeongeo tagi
자전거 타기

Taekwondo
Taekwondo
태권도
This martial art is the national sport of South Korea. Taekwondo is loosely translated as "the way of the foot and fist" or "the way of kicking and punching." The basics are taught beginning in elementary school—so don't mess with a Korean unless you wanna get your face broken.

Soccer
Chukgu
축구
Believe it or not, Korea is pretty badass at soccer. Not only did they host the 2002 World Cup, but they ranked fourth. The event brought the whole Korean community together, and everyone dressed in red to cheer for the team. It was common to sneak your own alcohol into the games and yell at the refs and opposing players. But Korean fans are pretty polite, in general.

Shoot!
Shoot!
슛!

Pass the ball!
Pass *jom hae!*
패스 좀 해!

Gooooooooal!
Goal~in!
골인!

Rec soccer team
Jogi chukguhoe
조기축구회
Some athletically inclined Korean men wake up before the crack of dawn to play soccer with other crazies—I mean other athletically inclined guys—before they all trudge off to work.

......Just dance
Chumchwo
춤춰

Dancing is really big in Korea, and TV stations feature a lot of popular dance shows. So you'd best bring your A-game if you're gonna hit the floor.

Let's **dance.**
Uri ***chumchuja.***
우리 **춤추자.**

You can't **dance for shit!**
Ireon ***momchi!***
이런 **몸치!**

Hey, don't **freestyle,** you look like an idiot!
Ya, ***makchum*** *chujima, eolgani gatah*
야, 막춤 추지마, 얼간이 같아!

I love...
Na ... joahae.
나 ... 좋아해.

ballet.
balleh
발레

B-boys.
B-boys
비보이즈
Break dancing wasn't popular in Korea until recently, but now it's huge, and Korean B-boys are some of the best in the world. International B-boy competitions are even held in Seoul.

There are many traditional Korean dances (*hanguk jeontong muyong;* 한국 전통 무용) that you may see while visiting.

Fan dance
Buchaechum
부채춤
During Korean festivals, female dance teams create beautiful flowers using their bodies and large feathered fans.

Mask dance
Talchum
탈춤
The mask dance is an example of the earliest Korean storytelling done through dance. This folk art is a theatrical production that traditionally features male performers—even for female roles. Check out the Korean film *The King and the Clown* (2005)—you'll be surprised how cute the guys can be in drag.

Sword dance
Kalchum
칼춤
Shamans perform this dance to summon spirits.

……Cheering

Eungwon

응원

Korean cheerleaders are a bit different from the American concept. Most strikingly, many of them are male, and they use drums and flags instead of booty shorts and fake tits to get the crowd pumped up. The most famous cheering supporters of the South Korean national football (soccer) team were the Red Devils from the 2002 World Cup. Korean fans amazed the world with their passion and also their orderliness after the games. Yup, that's right—Koreans can be orderly!

K-O-R-E-A
Dae-han-min-guk
대한민국

Keep fighting!
Hwaiting!
화이팅!

You're playing great!
Jalhanda!
잘한다!

It's okay!
Gwaenchana!
괜찮아!

Go, team!
Uritim jalhanda!
우리팀 잘한다!

We are the champions!
Uriga championiya!
우리가 챔피온이야!

The referee got paid off!
Simpansaekki don muggussuh!
심판새끼 돈먹었어!

Booing
Yayu hada
야유 하다

Boo!
Woo!
우!

This team blows!
I tim byeongsingata!
이 팀 병신같아!

We suck!
Uri jolla mothae!
우리 졸라 못해!

•••••Winter sports
Gyeoul sports
겨울 스포츠

The weather gets pretty cold during winter in Korea. Schools get about a month off for winter break, and that's the best time to enjoy winter sports such as snowboarding, skiing, skating, and sledding. The best places in Korea for winter activities are *Muju* (무주) and *Gangwondo* (강원도).

Let's ...
...tareo gaja.
... 타러 가자.

go snowboarding.
Snowboard
스노우보드

go skiing.
Ski
스키

go ice skating.
Ice skate
스케이트

go speed skating.
Spid skate
스피드 스케이트

Korean speed skate teams have been among the top competitors in the Olympics. Even the US team has hired former medalist Jae-su Chun as their head coach to enhance the performance.

go figure skating.
Figure skate
피겨 스케이트

Korea has been known mainly for its speed skaters, but lately the country has gained recognition in the figure-skating arena. Even before winning the 2010 Olympic gold medal, Yu-na Kim was making waves in international competitions. So now the whole world knows—Korea's number one!

1988 SEOUL OLYMPICS

PALPAL SEOUL OLYMPICS
팔팔 서울 올림픽

Palpal means "88" in Korean.

The 1988 Summer Olympics were held in Seoul. North Korea boycotted the event because it was still officially at war with South Korea. But the Games brought a lot of attention to South Korea and really promoted the country's image. They remain an important event in Korean history.

Hodori
Hodori
호돌이

Hodori was the name of the beloved, friendly-looking tiger mascot of the Seoul Olympics.

go sledding.
Sseolmae
썰매

•••••Fitness
Sinche dallyeon
신체 단련

Korean Standard National Exercise
Gukminchejo
국민체조
Developed by the South Korean government in the 1970s, *gukminchejo* is a 12-step series of stretches that every Korean kid does, starting in elementary school. And to keep the school day free for learning, these organized exercises are held before classes start. How thoughtful.

I'm too fat to do the long jump.
Nan jejari meollittwigi hagien neomu ttungttunghae.
난 제자리 멀리뛰기 하기엔 너무 뚱뚱해.

I can do 1,000...
Na ... 1,000 gae halsuisseo.
나 ... 1,000 개 할수있어.

pull-ups. (men)
teokgeori
턱걸이
In Korea, girls don't really do pull-ups, at least not during school fitness tests. The gender-specific exercise girls do is called *orae maedalligi* (오래 매달리기), which literally means "dangling." Girls hold the pull-up "up" position (chin above the bar) for as long as their skinny little arms can take it.

sit-ups.
witmom ireukigi
윗몸 일으키기

push-ups.
pal gupyeopigi
팔 굽혀펴기

Benching will get you huge **pecs.**
***Benching**hamyeon **geunyuk** eomcheongnajyeo.*
벤칭하면 **근육** 엄청나져.

You gotta do **squats** to hit the **glutes.**
***Dari gupigi**reul haeya **eongdeongi**ga olaga.*
다리굽히기를 해야 **엉덩이**가 올라가.

My **abs** are killing me!
***Bae** ttaengyeo jukkesseo!*
배 땡겨 죽겠어!

I'm getting **ripped!**
*Na wanjeon **ttanttanhaji**!*
나 완전 **딴딴하지**!

You're looking toned.
Mom jom joaboyeo.
몸 좀 좋아보여.

My whole body is sore.
Na on mom ssusyeo.
나 온 몸 쑤셔.

•••••Children's games
Aideul nori
아이들 놀이

Before the invention of addictive sedentary video games, there were simpler pastimes that kids enjoyed outside with their friends. With four beautiful and distinct seasons, Korea has always been a huge playground for kids.

MINI OLYMPICS OF KOREA FIELD DAY

UNDONGHOE

운동회

These mini-Olympics are conducted in elementary school and junior high. The whole school gets together, and entire families come out to cheer for their kids. It's a lesson in sportsmanship, because even when you're having fun, you're learning something. For children in Korea, the mini-Olympics are as important as the high school prom.

Dodgeball
Pigu
피구
Dodgeball is one of the most popular games in the mini-Olympics.

Here comes my fireball!
Ja-a, bulkkotshut badara!
자아, 불꽃슛 받아라!

Tug of war
Juldarigi
줄다리기

These are sounds you make when you pull the rope:
Eucha, eucha!
으차, 으차!
Yeongcha, yeongcha!
영차, 영차!

Relay
Relay/ieodalligi
릴레이 / 이어달리기

Korean piñata
Bakteoteurigi
박터트리기
Instead of taking turns hitting the piñata with a bat, there are separate piñatas for each team. Whoever throws enough bean bags to pop open the piñata is the winner.

Top (toy)
Paengichigi
팽이치기

Kite
Yeonnalligi
연날리기

Hacky sack
Jegichagi
제기 차기

Patty cake
Ssessesse
쎄쎄쎄

Hopscotch
Ttangttameokgi
땅따먹기

Gonggi
Gongi
공기
Gonggi is similar to jacks. It's played using five colored plastic tokens called *gongitdol*. Each player tosses the tokens on the ground and throws one into the air, then has to scoop up the ones on the ground and catch the airborne one. There are five levels, and players score points by tossing all five *gongitdol* and then catching them on the back of their hand. Play proceeds until the airborne token is dropped or other tokens are touched or moved unintentionally. It's mostly played at grade-school age.

Horseback game
Malttukbakki
말뚝박기
Sadly, this game doesn't involve an actual horse. It's a rough game mainly played by boys. Two teams are chosen, and one of them becomes the horse post. The "horses" make a chain by bending over and sticking their heads between their teammates' legs. The competing team then hops on the back of the other team without letting it fall apart. When all the teammates are on the competitors' backs, the team leader plays Rock Paper Scissors with the other team leader to decide who will be the winner. This is popular with everyone from children to university students.

•••••Traditional Korean games

Minsoknori

민속놀이

Yut board game

Yutnori

윷놀이

Yut is a board game about raising livestock that's usually played during the Korean New Year.

Korean cockfight

Dakssaum

닭싸움

It's not what you think, assuming you were thinking about chickens fighting each other to death. (If you weren't, you have a dirty, dirty mind and may be addicted to porn.) In the Korean cockfight, two people each stand on one leg and support their other leg with their hands. They hop toward each other and try to make their competitor be the first to let go of their leg.

Korean wrestling

Ssireum

씨름

Of course, there has to be a game where guys get worked up and show their strength. Like sumo wrestling, fat men in diapers rub against each other to knock the other guy down or out of the ring. The winner used to get a bull for his prize, so it was a big deal a long time ago. Now, not so much—it's a dying sport, cuz most of the athletes have moved on to mixed martial arts.

The Korean Wrestling Champion of the Year (the strongest man)
Cheonhajangsa
천하장사

Mock cavalry battle
Gimajeon
기마전
This is like a game you play in the pool, only on a mass scale. A group is divided into two teams to play a mock cavalry battle in which the "knights" ride on the shoulders of the "horses" who carry them to battle on the ground.

Korean chess
Jang-gi
장기
Jang-gi, derived from the Chinese game *xiangqi*, is a strategic board game that's popular in Korea and is sometimes referred to as Korean chess. The playing board is 9 lines wide by 10 lines long.

Checkmate!
Jangiyo!
장이요!

Go
Baduk
바둑
Featured in the movie *A Beautiful Mind*, Go is a board game noted for strategic complexity despite its simple rules. The world's Go champions have always been Koreans, not Japanese or Chinese. Perhaps it's time for the international name to be changed to Baduk!

Korean folded paper tiles flip game
Ddakji chigi
딱지치기
If you have seen *Squid Game*, you have seen a *ddakji*, which is a folded paper tile typically made out of newspapers or magazines. In order to score in a game of *ddakji chigi*, you have to flip your opponent's ddakji. Don't worry, slapping isn't involved unless you set that as a rule.

•••••Video games

Video game

비디오 게임

Have we mentioned that Korean kids (mostly boys) love to play video games? Guys can sit in front of their computers killing all those little monsters for days without much rest. The addiction is so extreme, it's even killed someone. No, not like the violent American who shot his mom in the head when she took away his Xbox. A Korean teenager was found dead after he locked himself in a room for a week. He played video games alone, without sleeping or eating, and his body eventually just stopped working from lack of nutrients and pure exhaustion. Other than that incident, video games can actually be good for stimulating your brain. Try to battle your way into the world of Korean gamers.

I can't wait to play the new...
Saero naon ... jeongmal hagosipeo.
새로 나온 ... 정말 하고싶어.

Lineage: The Blood Pledge.
리니지

In this popular online game, players can work their way to the pro leagues. They can become professional gamers and make up to $100,000 per year, sponsored by big corporations such as LG and Samsung.

World of Warcraft (WoW).
WoW game
와우 게임

Starcraft.
Starcraft
스타크레프트

PUBG: Battlegrounds.
Baetl geuraundeu
배틀그라운드

This game is often called *baegeu* (배그) for short.

The enemy is at 3 o'clock!
Jeogi saesi banghyange itda!
적이 3시 방향에 있다!

He's using a cheat key!
Chiteuki sseunda!
치트키 쓴다!

He's using wall hack!
Maphaek sseunda!
맵핵 쓴다!
This is an illegal cheat tool used in games, especially RTS or online games, to reveal hidden information like enemy locations or fog of war.

•••••Gambling
Dobak
도박

Seoul's got a gambling area, but Koreans aren't allowed in. Casinos are only for foreign visitors. So if you wanna be a high roller, you gotta bring your passport to get through the casino doors. Despite these restrictions, Koreans are still known as avid gamblers and can become highly addicted to betting it all. No worries, though; what they can't get in their own backyard is just a jet ride away in Las Vegas, which has become the all-time favorite tourist destination for Koreans.

Illegal gambling
Bulbeobdobak
불법도박

It's only illegal when you get caught gambling.
Dobageun hadaga japyeohsseulttae bulbeobiya.
도박은 하다가 잡혔을때 불법이야.

Bet
Geolgi
걸기

> **Do you want to bet money?**
> *Don **geollae**?*
> 돈 걸래?

Go-Stop
Go-Stop
고스톱
This game originated from similar games in Japan, using cards called Hwatoo. Three players and a banker play, and whoever collects the most matching cards wins the game.

Ah, I have the shitty card!
A, tto ssanne!
아, 또 쌌네!

You're short with your point!
Pibage gwangbagine!
피박에 광박이네!

Jeongseon City
Jeongseon
정선
This town is like the Korean Las Vegas, but strictly regulated. You're only allowed to visit three times a month. They check your ID and keep records on how much you spend. It's not nearly as glamorous as its American counterpart, and the only free drink you'll get is soda. They're trying to make it more fun by building new resorts, but if you're really itching to gamble, Seoul is still your best bet.

Horse racing
Gyeongma
경마
There's a limit on how much you can bet on a race, normally up to 500,000 won (about $350).

Bike racing
Gyeongryunjang
경륜장
Yes, there is bike racing that you can watch and bet on!

Bullfighting
Sossaum
소싸움
This is not like Spanish or Mexican bullfighting—no Korean is dumb enough to jump into a ring with a bull. Korean bullfighting, usually held in the countryside, pits two bulls against each other, but doesn't happen often these days.

CHAPTER 9

HUNGRY KOREAN

HANGUKESEO BAEGOPEULTTAE HANEUNMAL

한국에서 배고플때 하는말

If you're a vegetarian or vegan, don't come to Korea. Just don't. Korea is a meat country, and if you're not down with that, GTFO. Because of this carnivorous spirit, BBQ is big in Korea—and ridiculously delicious—but it can be pricey. This is mainly because Korean beef is almost three times more expensive than American beef. So you'll usually find pork served as the meat of choice at these restaurants. The best Korean BBQ comes from the little hole-in-the-walls found in any city. Be sure to check one out for an authentic Korean experience.

Even bigger than BBQ are pork belly slices (*samgyeopsal*; 삼겹살). Koreans just looooove these. And dog meat, though not eaten by most people and technically illegal, is still consumed by a small minority—which, though kind of disgusting, shows you just how much Koreans really, really love their meat.

Of course, man cannot live on meat alone. And that's where rice comes in. Despite a steady decline in the country's rice consumption, Koreans still eat just about everything with rice.

And by everything, I do mean everything. No matter what or when you're eating—be it breakfast, lunch, or dinner—it's gonna come with rice.

••••• Hunger

Baegopeum

배고픔

I'm starving.
Baegopa.
배고파.

I'm dying of hunger.
*Na **baegopa** jukkesseo.*
나 **배고파** 죽겠어.

I'm dying of thirst.
*Na **mok malla** jukkesseo.*
나 **목 말라** 죽겠어.

Let's eat!
Bab meokja!
밥 먹자!

I could go for some...
Na ... meokgosipeo.
나 ... 먹고싶어.

food.
eumsik
음식

chow.
meogeulkkeo
먹을거

drinks.
masilkkeo
마실거

beverages.
eumryosu
음료수

street food.
gilgeori eumsik
길거리 음식

junk food.
bullyang sikpum
불량식품

fast food.
fast food
페스트 푸드

sumptuous feast. (indicates a variety of dishes)
jinsuseongchan
진수성찬

good meal.
masinneun eumsik
맛있는 음식

healthy food.
geongangsik
건강식

Korean BBQ.
cheolpangui / sutbulgyi
철판구이 / 숯불구이

Koreans love beef and pork, but because beef is expensive, the most common meat at a Korean BBQ is pork. The phrases for Korean BBQ include terms like *cheolpan*, which means "metal grill," and *sutbul*, which means "charcoaled."

Chinese food.
Junguk eumsik
중국음식
You can also use the word *jjankkae* (짱개), which is slangier.

delivery service.
baedal
배달
Almost all restaurants in Korea will deliver takeout without any extra fee or tip. Most delivery boys use motorcycles fitted with stainless steel carriers called *cheolgabang* (철가방). These spacious cases with interior shelves for stacking plates are so synonymous with delivery service that the word has also become slang for the delivery guys.

all-you-can-eat buffet.
muhan refill
무한 리필
Some of these pig-out restaurants have a one-hour time limit. To get your money's worth, you'd better learn to quickly stuff your face. It's not so hard to eat fast in Korea, since everyone likes to get things done quickly.

I'm full.
Baebulleo.
배불러.

I'm stuffed to my neck.
Mokkaji kkwak chasseo.
목까지 꽉 찼어.

I'm going to throw up.
To nawa.
토 나와.

I'm going to burst.
Bae teojigesseo.
배 터지겠어.

Thanks for the meal. (said before the meal)
Jal meokkeseupnida.
잘 먹겠습니다.

It's considered polite to announce that you are thankful for the meal when someone buys you food.

Thanks for the meal. (said after the meal)
Jal meogeosseupnida.
잘 먹었습니다.

••••• Delicious
Jinjja masisseo
진짜 맛있어

Really tasty.
Mat jota.
맛 좋다.

It melts in my mouth.
Hyeoe salsal nokneunda.
혀에 살살 녹는다.
This is useful when you have really good sashimi.

It was really good.
Neomu masisseosseo.
너무 맛있었어.

Yum yum.
Yamyam jjeopjjeop.
얌얌 쩝쩝.

It's sweet and spicy.
Maekomhada.
매콤하다.

It warms up my body. (for hot soup)
Eolkeunhada.
얼큰하다.

Filling
Bae chewojinda
배 채워진다

I'm going to order more.
Chugayo.
추가요.

•••••Yuck!
Uek!
우엑!

Gross!
Deoreowo!
더러워!

This place sucks!
Yeogi mateopsseo!
여기 맛없어!

PICKY EATERS
PYEONSIK
편식

It's common for parents to nag their children into eating all their food, especially vegetables. These are some of the phrases you might hear as mothers attempt to coerce/guilt/scare their picky kids into eating what's good for them. You might also use it on your anorexic Korean girlfriend to get extra meat on her!

You will be punished if you don't finish your meal.
Eumsik namgimyeon beolbada.
음식 남기면 벌받아.

You won't grow if you don't eat this.
Neo igeo an meogeumyeon ki ankeunda.
너 이거 안 먹으면 키 안큰다.

Don't be picky—eat everything.
Neo pyeonsikhajimalgo golgoru meogeo.
너 편식하지말고 골고루 먹어.

What a waste of money.
Doni neomu akkapda.
돈이 너무 아깝다.

It's disgusting.
Igeo yeokgyeowo.
이거 역겨워.

It's dirty in there.
Geu gage jijeobunhae.
그 가게 지저분해.

It's so-so.
Geu gage geunyang geurae.
그 가게 그냥 그래.

It's too pricey and not good enough.
Bissagiman hae.
비싸기만 해.

••••• At the restaurant
Eumsikjeomeseo
음식점에서

Restaurant service in Korea is generally top-notch. And as a wallet-friendly bonus, the food is usually fairly affordable. You can get a gourmet, home-cooked meal for under $20. And the tax and tip are often included, as are constant refills of side dishes, called *banchan* (반찬). They also won't bring you the bill until you request it.

Another thing to remember: Don't sit around waiting for servers to take your order or clear your plate. You're expected to call them anytime you want them. Don't be a dick about it, though—call them *eonni* (언니; "sister") or *imo* (이모; "aunt") in a friendly way. And don't try to tip servers in Korea, because they might find it insulting. Also, don't be too picky about your food. Korean restaurants aren't like Burger King—you don't get to have it your way. They don't like to substitute or leave out ingredients for you. It's not common to ask for to-go or doggy bags, either.

Popular restaurant
Matjib
맛집
Instead of using Yelp to look for popular restaurants, Korean people use the Naver app to search for trending places to eat.

Excuse me!
Jeogiyo!
저기요!

Over here!
Yeogiyo!
여기요!
This is more common than "excuse me" for calling the wait staff. Servers in Korea won't come to you unless you raise your hand and yell to get their attention!

Can we order?
Jumuniyo.
주문이요.
Literally, "Get my order."

What do you recommend?
Yeogi moga jeil masisseoyo?
여기 뭐가 제일 맛있어요?

How much is this?
Igeo eolmayaeyo?
이거 얼마예요?

How big is the portion?
Yangi eottaeyo?
양이 어때요?

What's in this?
Yeogi moga deureoisseoyo?
여기 뭐가 들어있어요?

Can I get this?
Igeo juseyo.
이거 주세요.

Can I get a menu?
Menupan juseyo.
메뉴판 주세요.

Can I get some water?
Mul jom juseyo.
물 좀 주세요.

Give me my bill.
Gyesanseo juseyo.
계산서 주세요.

Let's go Dutch.
Dutch pay haja.
더치 페이 하자.

Older Koreans traditionally take the bills and pay for a whole table. However, the younger generation has adopted the custom of paying for oneself—mostly to save people from going broke. If you're taking a girl out on a date, though, don't be a cheapskate. Guys are still expected to treat.

•••••Popular Korean food
Hangukeui yumyeonghan yori
한국의 유명한 요리

We love Korean food, and it's not just because we're Korean. OK, maybe it is, but even non-natives will be amazed at the variety of offerings. The following are some of the tastiest and most popular dishes you'll encounter in your travels.

Rice
Bap
밥
White rice is the country's main staple and is served in most Korean restaurants. Rice is so integral to the Korean diet that it's also a synonym for "food."

Mixed-grain rice
Japgokbap
잡곡밥
If you visit your Korean friend's family, you'll likely be served a multigrain mix of rice.

Kimchi
Kimchi
김치
This is the most famous Korean side dish. Best known to Westerners is the fiery pickled-cabbage variety, but in reality there are more than 50 kinds of kimchi! Don't be afraid to try variations made with turnips, cucumbers, and onions—not all of them are spicy.

Ramen
Ramyeon
라면
Most Korean ramen consists of instant noodles that come in a variety of flavors. It's been said that one university student lived off ramen for a month and died from lack of nutrients, so I don't recommend eating too many packages. But it's good and cheap food for curing a hangover!

Udon
Udong
우동
This Japanese noodle soup is really popular in Korea.

Fried fish cakes
Odaeng
오뎅
Served on a stick, these fried fish cakes are some of the most popular street foods in Korea. You may also see a sliced version

show up in the myriad side dishes brought to the table at a Korean BBQ.

Seaweed rice roll
Kimbap
김밥
Kimbap is a Korean sushi roll. Mothers pack them for their children's field trips—or if you have a lazy mom, she'll give you the 1,500 won (about $1.20 given current exchange rate) that it costs to buy one.

Tempura
Twigim
튀김
Fried food is universally yummy. Even skinny Koreans can't resist the allure of these crispy, greasy treats.

Spicy rice cake
Ddeokbeokgi
떡볶이
This rice cake dish, flavored with *gochujang* (고추장)—a condiment made with red chilies and fermented soybeans—is perfect for large groups of people gathered at street vendors.

Pig-intestine noodles (Korean blood sausage)
Sundae
순대
It may sound gross, but this is one of the tastiest foods you may ever try. The sausage is stuffed with clear noodles, then soaked in pig's blood to give it a unique flavor. The dish also comes with a side of steamed pig's ears, intestines, and liver. Oink, oink!

Korean mixed rice
Bibimbap
비빔밥

Literally, "mixed rice." A combination of fresh vegetables and marinated meat with rice that you mix with *gochujang* (red chili paste).

Black bean noodles
Jjajangmyeon
짜장면
This dish uses the same fermented and salted black beans seen in Chinese cookery, but *jjajang* (짜장) served over noodles is much thicker than the Chinese version.

Spicy seafood noodle soup
Jjambbong
짬뽕
A spicy noodle soup with seafood, *jjambbong* is a Chinese-Korean dish served in all the Chinese restaurants in Korea.

Sushi
Chobap
초밥
Koreans typically like their sushi served nigiri style—raw fish over rice. However, ever since California rolls became popular here, Korean sushi chefs have invented a lot more fusion maki rolls (rice rolled around veggies or fish). How about maki sushi smothered in a sweet yogurt sauce? It just might be your next favorite thing to eat.

Sashimi
Hoe
회
Koreans use a spicy sauce called *chogouchujjang* (초고추장) for sashimi instead of the traditional wasabi.

Live sashimi
Hwareohoe
활어회
You choose a live fish from a tank outside the restaurant; the fish is then prepared for you on the spot. Expect a much thinner cut of sashimi than you're used to in the US—the fresh flesh is so chewy that a thicker slice would make it hard to eat.

Pho
Weolnam guksu
월남국수
Vietnamese rice noodle soup with sliced beef.

Korean ox bone soup
Seolleongtang
설렁탕
Oxtail soup is normally boiled for a day to extract all the rich calcium from the bone.

Pizza
Pizza
피자
If you're sick and tired of eating Korean BBQ with rice and are craving American food such as pizza, you might not get quite what you're looking for. Pizza in Korea is healthy compared to the US counterpart—it's less greasy and has more nutritious toppings, such as king shrimp, squid, and corn.

Pig's feet
Jokbal
족발

Boiled pig
Bossam
보쌈
Chinese cabbage is wrapped around tender broiled pork.

Dog stew
Bosintang
보신탕
The concept of dog stew sounds repugnant to Americans—to most Koreans, too. But those who do eat the canine concoction do so in the belief that it restores health, which is reflected in the dish's name. *Bosin* literally means "restoring health to the body." Today it's illegal to eat dog meat in Korea.

Sliced rice pasta soup
Tteokguk
떡국
This traditional rice cake soup is eaten on Lunar New Year's Day.

Dumpling soup
Manduguk
만두국

Soft tofu soup
Soondubu-jjigae
순두부
Soondubu-jjigae (pronounced "soon-doo-boo jee-gae") is a popular Korean stew made with extra-soft tofu (*soondubu*), a spicy broth, and usually seafood, meat (like pork or beef), or vegetables. It's served boiling hot in a stone pot, and often topped with a raw egg that cooks right in the soup.

Kimchi soup
Kimchijjigae
김치찌개
This spicy, savory dish is traditionally made with pork, but don't be surprised to see pink slices of SPAM floating in the broth when it's prepared by a home cook. Sounds kinda gross, but it's not. Who would have thought that kimchi and SPAM could go so well together?

Seaweed soup
Miyeokguk
미역국
Koreans always have this on their birthdays. Women who've just given birth also consume this tasty broth, which is high in calcium and iron. Presto—the association with birthdays!

Korean pancake
Buchimgae
부침개
This savory wheat-flour pancake is served as an appetizer or snack. It can include kimchi (surprise), green onions, or even squid. The plain ones with just green onions are called *pajeon* (파전); they're good topped with soy sauce.

Shaved ice
Patbingsu
팥빙수
Shaved ice with red bean sauce, topped with mochi balls and fruit—it's the bomb!

Fried chicken
Tongdak
통닭
We don't want to brag, but Koreans fry a motherfucking mean chicken! *Tongdak* (통닭) literally means "whole chicken" in Korean. It refers to a whole chicken that's deep-fried without being cut into pieces first—crispy on the outside, juicy on the inside. This is different from American-style fried chicken, which is usually cut into parts (like wings, thighs, drumsticks), coated in a batter or seasoned flour, and then fried. *Tongdak* usually skips the heavy breading and keeps things simple but flavorful!

K-fried chicken
Chikin
치킨
Korean fried chicken isn't just regular fried chicken—it's next-level. What makes it special is the thin, ultra-crispy skin (thanks to double-frying!) and the signature sauces, like sweet and spicy yangnyeom or soy-garlic glaze. It's lighter and crunchier than American-style fried chicken, and it's often paired with pickled radish and beer—aka chimaek (chicken + maekju = beer).

•••••Fast food
Fast food
패스트 푸드

Bunsikjeom
분식점
These Korean fast-food restaurants are like gourmet ampms. You can get food freshly cooked right in front of you or just pick up some convenient and cheap prepackaged Korean grub.

McDonald's
맥도날드

KFC
케이에프씨

Burger King
버거킹

Popeyes
파파이스

Lotteria
롯데리아
This burger franchise is the McDonald's of Korea.

Kimbapcheonguk
김밥천국
Quick, cheap Korean food is served by this popular chain.

Kyochon Chicken
교촌치킨
Chicken with sweet and spicy seasoning is the specialty of this popular franchise.

bb.q Chicken
비비큐치킨
I'm not a big fried-chicken fan, but damn, this is legit!

Mr. Pizza
미스터 피자
The most famous pizza chain in the country, Mr. Pizza has a nice native twist—it has a sweet potato crust.

Red Mango
레드 망고
Italy has their gelato. Americans have their ice cream. Koreans have their frozen yogurt. Red Mango is the best-known of Korean yogurt chains and has even become successful in the US.

•••••Cafés

Cafe

카페

Cafés in Korea are fancy. American franchises such as Starbucks are just like the ones in the US, but you'll find some Korean twists at native coffeehouse chains—latte flavors such as sweet potato and green tea cater to a decidedly Asian palate.

Should we go to a coffee shop to talk?
Uri coffee shope gaseo yaegihalkka?
우리 커피숍에 가서 얘기할까?

Let's go to a...
... gaja.
... 가자.

Starbucks.
Starbucks
스타벅스
Koreans also call this *byeoldabang* (별다방), literally meaning "star coffee shop." It's also called *seubuck* (스벅) for short.

Coffee Bean.
Coffee Bean
커피빈
Sometimes this shop is just called *kongdabang* (콩다방), literally meaning "bean coffee shop."

ACKNOWLEDGMENTS

I would like to thank my editor, Kierra Sondereker, for reaching out to me to update this book. It's been more than 10 years since I first wrote it, and I recognize the need to update some old slang to keep up with Gen Zs.

I feel lucky to be able to work with my sister Jinny as coauthor for this edition. She is married, has a child, and is still hilarious and keeps up with trends.

Lastly, I thank you, the readers. I know you are in awe of the charming K-drama actors and K-pop idols. I hope you can learn how to say "I love you!" or "Make me your sex slave" when you come to visit South Korea and run into celebrities!

—Haewon Baek

I would like to thank my sister and Ulysses Press for giving me the chance to coauthor this book. It was surreal working together with my sister across the ocean in completely different time zones. I hope the K-culture loving readers enjoy this book and laugh along.

—Jinny Baek

ABOUT THE AUTHORS

Haewon Baek was born and raised in Seoul, South Korea. At the age of 13, she immigrated with her family to the United States, where she not only gained an affinity for American culture but also learned that when words like "ass" and "fuck" are used in the right order, they garner great attention. Haewon currently lives in Colorado with her husband and three children and works as a psychotherapist in a private practice. She visits her sister Jinny, coauthor of this book, in Jeju, Korea, during her kids' summer break so that she can continue to be engaged in K-culture.

Haejin Baek, also known as Jinny Baek, is the adventurous older sister of Haewon Baek. Originally a Seoulite, she seamlessly transitioned to American life at 14 when her family relocated. Excelling in her studies, she double-majored in English literature and TESOL, eventually returning to Korea to immerse herself in its culture as an English teacher at middle schools. What was meant to be a year's sabbatical turned into a lifelong love affair with Korea, complete with a charming Korean husband and a delightful son. Now settled on the enchanting island of Jeju, she passionately teaches English to Koreans of all ages, from lively youngsters to eager adults. She's also working as a mini-influencer in Korea as Mom.glish, helping Korean moms expose their kids to English and teaching them English expressions to use with their crazy kids in their daily lives. You can find her on Instagram @mom.glish.